Frontier Meditat___
Historians on the West and Writing, 2017-2023

By Erik J. Wright

Frontier Meditations:
Historians on the West and Writing, 2017-2023

ISBN: 9798866783519

ASIN: B0CN5BF62N

© Erik J. Wright, 2023. All Rights Reserved.

FIRST EDITION

Tripaw Press

Tripaw Press – Paragould, Arkansas

Printed in the United States of America

No part of this book may be reproduced without the express written permission of the author. There exists an exception for scholarly study for the use of articles, papers, and/or books in which the book is properly cited.

Published with the permission of the Wild West History Association *Journal* and *The Tombstone Epitaph* in which these interviews originally ran from 2017-2023.

www.tombstoneepitaph.com | www.wildwesthistory.org

**For my uncle, Bobby Jack Wright -
Westerner, outlaw, savior.**

"Presume not that I am the thing I was."

Henry IV Part Two
Act Five, Part One

"Remember the days of old; consider the years of many generations; ask your father, and he will show you, your elders, and they will tell you."

Hebrews 11:3

Preface

The idea for these interviews was first spawned when, in 2017, newly-appointed *The Tombstone Epitaph* editor Mark Boardman asked me to join him as his assistant editor. We knew there were many changes that needed to be made to the publication, but we dared not make them all at once. One change that was implemented soon after our "takeover" was the addition of author interviews. This was something that, to our knowledge, had not been done before in *The Tombstone Epitaph*. We made every attempt to run these interviews concurrently with book reviews which I also generally oversaw the production of. These interviews were done with established scholars of the West and, at times, emerging scholars. They always provided new and fresh insight into the world of how Western historians functioned in an increasingly modern society that seemed to care little about our frontier heritage.

What emerged from these interviews, that later were picked up as a new section in the Wild West History Association (WWHA) *Journal*, was a revelation for not only our readers, but for fellow historians and me. I found that in talking with these individuals I was consistently mentored by the best in the field. Sometimes, I was able to offer my own advice and experiences to them. It was my distinct honor to interview friends and longtime collaborators like Sam Dolan, Mike Bell, Peter Brand, Gary Roberts, and Casey Tefertiller. During the process, I made new ones like Richard Etulain, Jerome Greene, Matt Fitzsimons, Matthew Hulbert, James B. Mills, and Matt Bernstein. I also sadly was the last to interview the great

Robert Utley and Robert DeArment. May their works live on, but their candid insight into their careers and advice for future historians still are the legacy of this book.

Many of the historians featured in this book have published more books and papers since their interviews have been originally published in *The Tombstone Epitaph* or the WWHA *Journal*, but it was my intention to run the interviews as they originally appeared between the years 2017 and 2023. Little editing was done when the interviews initially appeared in an effort to retain the voice of the interviewee and therefore, I have carried that over to this volume. Only when necessary grammatical errors needed to be corrected did I intervene.

At times some interviews will feature brackets with information inside. That is my voice. But parentheses are the voice of the interviewee.

Author's Note: "West" denotes a place or theme while "west" denotes a direction.

Contents

Preface / 1
Samuel K. Dolan / 2
Anne F. Hyde / 6
Bill Betenson / 11
Bill Cavaliere / 15
Casey Tefertiller / 20
Chuck Parsons / 25
David A. Wolff / 29
Dennis Larsen / 38
Jerry Enzler / 42
Julia Bricklin / 49
Elliott West / 53
James B. Mills / 60
Jean Johnson / 67
John Boessenecker / 72
Kurt House / 76
Matthew Luckett / 81
Matthew Bernstein / 90
Matthew Hulbert / 96
Mark Boardman / 105
Roy B. Young / 109
Robert K. DeArment / 113
Sandy Barnard / 117
Patricia Tyson Stroud / 124
Brooks Blevins / 127
Norman W. Brown / 132
Michael Wallis / 136
Terry Smyth / 141
Anita H. Hernández / 147
Robert M. Utley / 151
Dan Buck / 156
Robert Watt / 161
Garner A. Palenske / 169
Bob Boze Bell / 174
Gary L. Roberts / 178

Peter Brand / 192
Richard W. Etulain / 200
Jerome A. Greene / 208
Michael Hiltzik / 212
Charles Rankin / 217
David D. de Haas / 222
B.J. Hollars / 231
Daniel J. Burge / 237
Bradley G. Courtney / 244
Larry D. Ball / 248
Linda Wommack 253
Mike Mihaljevich / 256
Mike Bell / 262
Matt Fitzsimons / 267
Acknowledgements / 273
About the Author / 274

Samuel K. Dolan is a historian, documentary writer, director, and Emmy Award-winning producer. Dolan, who grew up in Northern Arizona, got his start in the entertainment industry at the age of 13 when he spent the summer of 1993 riding horses on the set of the feature film *Tombstone*. Throughout the 1990s and early 2000s, Dolan appeared as an actor or double in many films and television shows before embarking on a career in documentaries. Since 2004, he has produced dozens of programs for History Channel, Military Channel, and National Geographic. In 2008, Dolan was the recipient of an Emmy Award for his work as producer on History Channel's *A Distant Shore: African-Americans of D-Day*. Between 2010 and 2012, Dolan helped develop a series for National Geographic called *Navajo Cops*, which he also directed. Dolan has also appeared as an on-camera expert on the History Channel and the American Heroes Channel. He currently lives in Montana with his wife and son.

EW (Erik Wright): Your debut book, *Cowboys and Gangsters: Stories of an Untamed Southwest* (TwoDot, 2016) offers a unique look at the rise of modern law enforcement at the close of the American frontier. What attracted you to this era that is often overlooked by other scholars?

SKD (Samuel K. Dolan): Growing up in Yavapai County, Arizona in the 1980s and 1990s I fell in love with the history of the Wild West at an early age, but there was something about that period after 1910 that really fascinated me. When I was a kid my dad and I would do our laundry in Clarkdale, and we would have dinner in a café right across the street from where lawman Jim Roberts shot it out with a pair of bank robbers in 1928. I loved that! That idea of an old timer from the 1880s who still packed a "Peacemaker" and took on a couple of modern-day crooks. I also loved westerns like *The Professionals* and *The Wild Bunch*. I read stories about Frank Hamer, Dave Allison, and Harry Wheeler. Finally, I think it was the experience I had while producing "Navajo Cops" for National Geographic that really made me realize that the west is still wild.

EW: Did the Wild West end at midnight on December 31, 1899?

SKD: Absolutely not! There's this rigid idea that American history plays out like a greatest hits album. One track ends and then another begins. I disagree with that. Look at the story of the Arizona Rangers. Crime was so bad in Arizona Territory in 1901 that a special force of lawmen was called upon to help tame a territory that was really only superficially "modern" and was still as lawless as Hell. Look at the raids across the border during the Mexican Revolution. Do you think anyone living out there at the time thought their world was any less "wild?" And then there's prohibition, which comes to the Southwestern states ahead of the 18th Amendment and produces basically a nearly two-decade long battle between lawmen and bootleggers. Many of the officers that shot it out with liquor runners and drug smugglers in the 1920s had also chases cattle rustlers and other bandits in the 1890s. Sure, they had automobiles, but the environment they worked in was really very much the same.

EW: In your opinion, who were some of the more intriguing figures to have emerged out of this period of transition?

SKD: Well, the most obvious one is Frank Hamer, a Texas Ranger that made the transition between horseback and automobile. Captain John R. Hughes would be another as his very notable career with the Rangers spanned the late 1800s and early 1900s. Of course, one of my favorite peace officers is an El Paso lawman named Charles E. Matthews, "The Australian Billy Smith." He was an Aussie prizefighter that joined the El Paso Police Department in the 1890s and was a lawman for almost 40 years. He even served in the Texas Rangers at one point. A very colorful figure that knew how to use his fists and rarely packed a gun. He spent a lot of years as a detective… a sort of Sherlock Holmes figure.

EW: What many people probably don't know is that you were in the movie *Tombstone*. Tell us about that experience.

SKD: With some help from some good friends in Arizona in the spring of 1993 my dad was hired as one of Peter Sherayko's "buckaroos" to work on *Tombstone*. That summer when I finished the 7th grade I went down to Tucson and got hired on as an extra and then later as a buckaroo. What a grand experience that was! Hell of a summer vacation! My first day on set I played a stable hand that takes Kurt Russell's horse at the train station. He tips me a dollar and says, "Easy on the grain, Butch." I spent the rest of the summer down there and it was one of the great adventures of my youth.

EW: Did your early work in the film industry have an impact in your interest in the American West as you grew older?

SKD: The *Tombstone* experience, followed by jobs on *Maverick* and TV shoots throughout High School led to work in documentary television. In my 20s I became a producer and worked mainly for History Channel,

Discovery, and other cable networks. I wrote a lot of WWII shows and that got me started as a writer and is how I established myself. So yes, there's a direct line between my love of the west, Tombstone, my television career, and writing.

EW: Discuss your latest book which you are now working on.

SKD: My current project is called *Hell Paso*. Basically, I am writing an overview of law and order and violence in El Paso between 1880 and 1920, so there's some overlap there with my first book. There are a lot of familiar figures of course, including Wes Hardin and John Selman, but I am really excited about the lesser-known characters and stories I get to dig into.

EW: Do you believe some of the stories in *Hell Paso* will be timely given the current geopolitical nature of the borderlands?

SKD: Yes, I certainly do believe the book will resonate with readers given the current issues about the border. While not every gunfight was a clash over race and culture, many of them were. The later chapters will cover the violence of the Revolution-era, Prohibition, and the start of the drug war, which began a lot earlier than most people think.

Anne F. Hyde is a professor of history at the University of Oklahoma, Anne Hyde also serves as the editor of the Western Historical Quarterly the publication of the Western History Association. A prize-winning historian with the Bancroft Prize for her 2011 book *Empires, Nations, and Families: A History of the North American West, 1800–1860*. Hyde has also written extensively on the frontier movement in the 19th-century.

EW (Erik Wright): Your new book helps to shed new light on the settlement of the West by bridging gaps in research of mixed ancestry. Describe your interest in this project and what compelled you to write the book.

AFH (Anne F. Hyde): When I was doing the research for my last book, *Empires, Nations, and Families*, which focused on the whole West between 1800 and 1860, I kept finding mixed-descent families running businesses, staffing forts, guiding, and advising western explorers, and serving in the U.S. Army. These families were everywhere, but by 1900 that proud mixing became illegal and a shameful heritage that people hid. Understanding how race works in U.S. culture seems to be the itch I can't stop scratching, so I began this project with two driving questions.

First, I needed to figure out where these families came from and why all this mixing started. Focusing on the long history of the fur trade seemed a good place to start. The largest set of business records in eighteenth and nineteenth-century North America details the fur trade. If you look carefully, those materials expose the daily decisions that built a business marrying European and Indigenous practices. Re-reading those records allowed me to explore how and where Indigenous and European communities made families and how they used kin to thrive on rivers that linked the fur trade and North America for nearly three hundred years.

Second, how could this long story of family-making help tribal nations and indigenous America now? Bitter divisions over tribal membership, blood quantum, and Native people's rights to define who they are roil Indian communities today. Now intermarriage could destroy Indigenous nations because it can reduce "blood quantum," that measure invented by racist scientists to eliminate Native people and to root mixed blood out of U.S. society.

EW: Were marriages between those of different races during the conquest of the west something out of necessity?

AFH: To understand all this, we need to think about both marriage and race a little differently. For most people, marriage has always been about diplomacy and increasing family resources. So, whether you were an English princess from marrying a Spanish prince or a Southern Cheyenne or Cayuse woman marrying a French or Anglo-American trader, the consideration was about benefits for your family or clan.

EW: What challenges did the couples and families of mixed cultures and races face during this era? How did each respective society come to accept them if at all?

AFH: Marrying across cultural differences was a common native strategy to replace lost warriors, increase allies, or make better trade deals. Many native groups had clans and ceremonies to make new and different people into kin. Until the late 1700s, French, British, and Spanish legal and church law encouraged intermarriage as long as it benefitted those communities and people married in the church and baptized their children. The trouble began in the 19th century and as the new United States began expanding and making treaties to end Native control over land. Then it became essential to define who was white, who was Native, and who could own property or who needed to be removed. The long history of mixed-descent families mixed up any clarity about all those racial lines. So, a woman like Mary Jane Drips, born into a Rocky Mountain fur trade family in 1824, was Otoe and Irish American. She spent her life fighting with the U.S. government and with Otoe tribal councils to protect her children and land into the early 1900s.

EW: Give some examples of the types of mixed-race marriages. Was it as simple as white and indigenous or did it become more complicated as westward expansion grew?

AFH: The book follows five families who all marry for different reasons. They had very different experiences in life. Some are extremely successful, some are failures, some choose to move into western cities, and others live on reservations. Many people in the fur trade, and in the communities surrounding the fur trade, married for diplomatic and practical reasons. So, if you were white St. Louisan William Bent and you were beginning the bison hide and alcohol trade in the 1830s, you needed a powerful connection to local people. Was it wise to marry into the Southern Cheyenne nation who had more recently moved to the southern plains or into the Comanche nation, the most powerful group in the region? Bent married the three daughters of an important Southern Cheyenne leader in 1836, and Owl Woman, Island, and

Yellow Woman raised five Bent children along the Arkansas River.

EW: What about the children of these couples? How did they find their identity as they grew into society?

AFH: This is complicated and very, very personal. Mixed-descent families had access to educations, language, and resources that not all their Native kin had. When Native nations had their cattle, horses, bison, and land stolen over the course of the nineteenth century, fights over dwindling resources made tribal politics bitter. Who was full-blood and who was mixed-blood now divided tribes in ways that gave race and blood power that they never had. Children from these families had to figure out how to be good kin in very difficult situations.

EW: Aside from your role as professor of history at the University of Oklahoma you also serve as editor-in-chief of the *Western Historical Quarterly*, the publication for the distinguished Western History Association (WHA). Can you talk about your role within the WHA and the association itself?

AFH: I've been editor of the *Western Historical Quarterly* since 2016. Watching the expanding range of scholarship about the west and its people and who writes and reads it is very exciting. Because the *WHQ* is the official publication of the Western History Association, it is my job to see that the journal reflects the interests of our members. They are younger and from a wider range of institutions and experience than the WHA I joined! I'm amazed every day by what appears in my inbox and actual book boxes on our office floor.

EW: Your 2012 book *Empires, Nations, and Families: A History of the North American West, 1800-1860* won that year's Bancroft Prize and the Caughey Western History Prize. It was also a Pulitzer Prize finalist in history. Many historians do not see their work recognized past the point of publication so describe the feelings you had to be honored in such a manner for your research.

AFH: Let's just say that was all a big surprise. It did give me the chance to talk about western issues and people that I really care about to a wider audience. Fewer people can dismiss frontiers and what happened to them as irrelevant. And all that attention certainly made it harder to write something else!

EW: Lastly, what advice do you wish to pass along to the next generation of western historians?

AFH: Be proud of the complicated place and history we share. Seeing and protecting such a complex and fragile past requires us to talk about and to learn to live with contested histories and landscapes. That is the work of many lifetimes.

Bill Betenson, who, at four-years-old, attended a screening of *Butch Cassidy and the Sundance Kid*. He saw the film with his great-grandmother, Lula Betenson, who wrote the book *Butch Cassidy, My Brother* in 1975. In the decades since, Bill Betenson has researched the life and times of his notorious ancestor using privileged family information and artifacts which culminated with the book *Butch Cassidy, My Uncle*. His latest book, *Butch Cassidy: The Wyoming Years*, was published in 2020.

EW (Erik Wright): Your great-grandmother, Lula Parker Betenson, wrote Butch Cassidy, My Brother in 1975. Why was it time for your family to pick up the subject of Butch Cassidy again?

BB (Bill Betenson): For me I have always been interested in Butch Cassidy. I grew up hearing stories from Lula and others and was always fascinated by him, so I have stuck with it more that probably anyone in the family so after spending 30 years researching him, I thought it was time to put some of the things I have found in writing for at least the family and other that are interested.

EW: How did Robert LeRoy Parker become Butch Cassidy?

BB: I think it was an evolution over time. He started out working outside his own family ranch for other area ranches for additional income for the family and there were things going on at some of the ranches for example the Jim Marshall ranch had rustling going on and he got involved in that. Over time he graduated to bigger things, and I think got hooked on the thrill and adrenaline involved in robberies. He always loved horses and became a great judge of fine flesh which in their day were the hot rods. He was a thinker and enjoyed planning robberies so they would be successful. I think he perfected the idea of relays of fresh horses to outdistance the posses and with his personality and love of people he made friends easily and instilled loyalty in folks who would hide him out which led to success overtime.

EW: Butch Cassidy is known around the world as one of the most noted outlaws the West ever produced. Do you see him differently considering your relationship to him?

BB: I think so. He is family and it is more personal. It obviously was very personal and hard on his parents and siblings. It was a big embarrassment that wasn't talk much outside the family. Enough time has passed now that it's just a fun family history. But I knew his sister well (I was 15 when she passed away) so I feel like a have a real tie that is tangible to him. I also talked to a great uncle that saw him and so growing up with these ties and spending time as a kid on the family ranch made it more tangible to me.

EW: Your latest book, *Butch Cassidy: The Wyoming Years*, work to unravel the myths and misconceptions of Cassidy. What are some examples of these?

BB: Butch legitimately tried to be a rancher in Wyoming. He had put together some stock (horses and cattle) and the stock were essentially stolen from him by the Embar Cattle Ranch run by Jay L. Torrey. Torrey tried to put Butch away for a long time and tried to prevent his pardon.

Butch was liked and respected by men on both sides of the law. The men who signed his petition for pardon is quite impressive (Judge, Senator, Mayor, Sheriff, etc). Wyoming really played such a pivotal role in the development of Butch Cassidy the outlaw.

EW: What turned Cassidy toward a life of outlawry?

BB: I think growing up poor and wanting more. He saw his father worked all his life for a ranch that didn't provide a whole lot. He saw an opportunity to get money in a way that brought some excitement and danger but offered potentially big rewards. After his prison term for something he likely was not guilty of (purchasing stolen horses, but not stealing the horses) I think he felt that if they were going to label him an outlaw, he would show them what a real outlaw was and because the leader of outlaws.

EW: Is there a consensus within your family about what happened to Cassidy?

BB: Definitely. Most believe he survived South America and came home to visit the family.

EW: Your great-grandmother passed away at the age of 96 in 1980. What was her opinion on the Paul Newman and Robert Redford film *Butch Cassidy and the Sundance Kid*?

BB: She liked it. She thought it captured the essence and character of Butch and his fun personality. She saw it 7-8 times. But said she did not believe his ending came in a shootout in Bolivia and if she did, she couldn't have watched it more than once.

She met the stars and was a good friend for many years to Robert Redford. They flew her back East for the premiere which she enjoyed.

EW: Butch Cassidy had a younger outlaw brother that many people don't know about. How was he?

BB: Yes, Butch's next youngest brother Dan Parker who was about 18 months younger than Butch. He was involved in a stage robbery in Wyoming and because they got into the U.S. Mail it led to a life sentence in a federal prison in Michigan since Wyoming at the time did not hold federal prisoners. It took a presidential pardon to get him released. Grover Cleveland denied his pardon, but William McKinley granted it at Christmas time after he had served nearly 8 years. He came home and didn't want anything to do with the outlaw life. He married and had a large family and lived in Southern Utah. Lula did not mention him in her book because of his descendants and did not want to bring any shame to them. But at this point they just want to know more about him.

My research shows that he played a minor role in the Telluride bank robbery, manning a relay of horses for the getaway.

EW: If Butch Cassidy was alive today, what would he think of all this attention? What one question would you want to ask him?

BB: I think he would get a kick out of it and probably laugh about it.

Just one question would be hard to decide. I'd like to sit down and have a long conversation about many things. But one question would be about why they went back into robbing in Argentina after establishing a legitimate ranch. I wonder if he missed the excitement?

Bill Cavaliere first moved to the Portal area of southeast Arizona where he we was employed with the U.S. Forest Service in the Chiricahua Mountains. Later, he moved into law enforcement and is the former sheriff of Hidalgo County, New Mexico. Today, Cavaliere is president of the Cochise County Historical Society and sits on the board of the Arizona Historical Society. His new book, *The Chiricahua Apaches: A Concise History*, is the result of a lifelong fascination of the people in the region he calls home.

EW (Erik Wright): Who were the Chiricahua Apaches?

BC (Bill Cavaliere): The Chiricahua Apaches are the descendants of a group that migrated from Asia approximately 10,000 years ago, crossing the Bering Land Bridge into Alaska and then continuing south, terminating in northern Mexico. Anthropologists believe they arrived in southwestern US and Mexico around 1200-1300 AD. Other tribes that derived from this original group were the Mescaleros, Navajos, Lipan. Jicarilla, Western and Kiowa Apaches. All are Athabaskan-speaking peoples, a language closely related to the Chipewyan, which is found in the sub-arctic regions of the far north. Because of this, many Apache words are like words spoken by the Inuits of Alaska and northern Canada. The Chiricahua Apaches were further divided into four bands: the Chokonen (Red Cliff People), Bedonkohe (Earth They Own It People), Nednhi (Enemy People) and Chihennes (Red Paint People). All four bands lived in different areas of the Chiricahua's homelands, which were called Apacheria.

EW: What drove the Apache to a lifestyle of warfare against the Americans and Mexicans?

BC: The Chiricahua Apaches originally were not a cruel or warlike tribe. It was only after they had been abused or betrayed that they retaliated in this manner. The Apaches had been at war with the Mexicans from the time of their arrival in the area. There were many instances of treachery and betrayal on the part of Mexicans against the Apaches dating back so far that it is impossible to locate the first incident. Historian Ed Sweeney calls the Apache's feelings toward Mexicans "fanatical hatred." When whites began arriving in the southwest, the Chiricahuas were originally friendly towards them. However, this all changed after the infamous Bascom Affair of 1861.

EW: Talk about your interest in this subject. How did you first become interested in Apache history?

BC: I lived for many years in southwest New Mexico and southeast Arizona, so I had always heard of Cochise, Geronimo, and Mangas Coloradas. But it took one incident many years ago, when I was day-working for a rancher friend of mine that really piqued my interest. We were diving in his pickup in Skeleton Canyon to gather some cattle. He pointed to a corral and told me that the big pile of rocks in it was the historic site where Geronimo had surrendered. From that point on, I wanted to learn everything about the Chiricahua Apaches.

EW: Your new book, *The Chiricahua Apaches: A Concise History*, was just released. What prompted you to begin such an ambitious project?

BC: been many books written on the Chiricahua Apaches; some biographies, some personal accounts, some relating to their culture, etc. But there are only a few that attempt to cover their whole story: Dan Thrapp's *The Conquest of Apacheria* and Ed Sweeney's *From Cochise to Geronimo* are some that come to mind. While all these books are excellent, I wanted to write a similar book, but one that flowed from one major incident to the next while leaving out minor details. This would make it easier to follow the significant events that occurred. I also wanted it to have interesting photographs, both historic as well as color photos of historic sites as they look today. Lastly, I had some new material that had never been published before.

EW: What are some common myths and misconceptions and the Chiricahua Apaches?

BC: Like I mentioned earlier, some think that the Chiricahua Apaches were always cruel, violent, and warlike. Again, this was only after they were forced to go into war. They had strong family bonds and were also a spiritual people. Also, the Hollywood image always seemed to portray Apaches as quiet and serious, when they laughed a lot and enjoyed joking around. Another common misconception is that Geronimo was a chief, a myth that I address in the book.

EW: Geronimo was arguably the most famous of all the Apaches. Following his surrender in 1886, what role did he have within the tribe as a prisoner of war?

BC: Geronimo was considered a medicine man by the Apaches and was believed to have strong Power. For this reason, he was frequently called upon for healing Apaches who were sick. At Mount Vernon Barracks, he was made a school disciplinarian and appointed Justice of the Peace.

However, many fellow Apaches blamed Geronimo for the predicament they were in as Prisoners of War. When Geronimo first arrived at Mount Vernon Barracks, none of his fellow Apaches, who had arrived there long before him, came out to greet him. Even today, most Chiricahua Apaches I have talked to do not speak highly of Geronimo.

EW: Let's discuss the notion that some Apaches fled to Mexico's Sierra Madres and never surrendered. Does this hold merit? If so, can we still identify Apache people in Mexico today?

BC: It certainly does hold merit. In fact, three historians are currently writing books on this subject: Alicia Delgadillo, Berndt Kuhn, and Lynda Sanchez. We know for a fact that a small group of Apaches changed their minds after the September 1886 surrender and escaped during the night back to Mexico. They consisted of two warriors, three women, one boy and one baby. In addition, it's my belief that other Apaches who were in Mexico never came in for the surrender. They may have known about it but decided to remain in hiding, or they may have been in some remote area of the Sierra Madres and didn't even know about the surrender. The late Ed Sweeney disagreed with me on this and felt that every Apache had turned themselves in and was accounted for, and we ended up in a friendly argument on this subject. Berndt Kuhn agrees with Ed. But I think there were just too many of these "Bronco Apaches," who raided up into the 1930s, to have originated from just those original seven escapees. As far as identifying any in Mexico today, I feel that all these Bronco Apaches are long dead. However, there no doubt are descendants of them through intermarrying with Mexicans.

I think that a Chiricahua Apache would be better suited to answer this question, but in my opinion, the Chricahuas of today are seen as both astute in business as well as traditionalists. Although they are a divided tribe, with some living near Fort Sill, Oklahoma and the others near Mescalero, New Mexico, they own such business investments as the Inn of the Mountain Gods in Mescalero, as well as the Apache Homelands restaurant and soon-to-be casino in Deming, NM. These are businesses that people of all races can enjoy. They also recently opened an office in Silver City, New Mexico, and own land near the Cochise Stronghold over by the Dragoon Mountains of Arizona. I think it's safe to say that they see themselves as growing and are taking steps to provide for expansion. Yet many Chiricahuas still practice their ancient traditions and speak their language, ensuring that their culture doesn't die. That's very admirable.

Casey Tefertiller is a former writer for the *San Francisco Examiner*. He is well-known for his groundbreaking biography, *Wyatt Earp: The Life Behind the Legend* and has recently co-edited *A Wyatt Earp Anthology: Long May His Story Be Told*. Tefertiller, now a renowned historian, was instrumental in dismantling the layers of misinformation written by the late Glenn Boyer which revolutionized the field of Earp studies.

EW (Erik Wright): We all know popular image of Wyatt Earp. But who was he really?

CT (Casey Tefertiller): Earp as a man was hard to know. He was quiet, almost dour. But he loved to laugh. His wife, Sadie, could entertain him and make him laugh. He participated in those practical jokes with Bat Masterson. He was often naive and too trusting of the likes of Johnny Behan. He was never the plaster saint of fiction. He was very human. He made mistakes and poor decisions. After being sober in Tombstone, he drank too much later in life. As with most people, he was very human. What separated him was his remarkable courage.

EW: What drew you into his story?

CT: When I was a child, my grandfather and I would sit and watch the reruns of the old Wyatt Earp TV show before dinner. My grandfather, Orie Dunlap, had been a working cowboy, then later a chief of Police. When he was in the bunkhouses, some of the old Arizona cowhands drifted into California and told stories about Earp and Tombstone. The stories they told made Earp into one of the great villains of the West. I would watch the TV show, then listen to my grandfather relate the stories he had heard. I was fascinated that one man could have such a divergent legacy — hero or villain? From the time I was a child, I wondered which it was. I set off to find out. What I found was certainly not what I expected.

EW: Some years ago you were very involved in dismantling the false narratives created by the late Glenn G. Boyer who had authored many books on Earp and his story. What have we learned about Earp since that time now the slate has been wiped clean?

CT: Imagine the concept: you have one of the most famous men in American history, and we are virtually starting over in understanding his life and legacy. Stuart Lake heroized Earp, then Frank Waters created a villain. Both included vast falsehoods. Then Boyer came along with his imaginary history. With the rubbish cleared away, there has been a new generation of research, with so many excellent historians working to find true history to fill the gaps. It has truly been an amazing last quarter-century in putting together new information and gaining a better understanding of the incredible Tombstone story.

EW: What challenges did you face in writing your groundbreaking 1997 biography *Wyatt Earp: The Life Behind the Legend*?

CT: This would take a book-length response. When I started, I was told it would be impossible to write an Earp biography — that everything important had already been found and only John Gilchriese or Boyer had access to critical information. Two writers called the publisher to try and prevent publication of my book. I drew up a hold-harmless absolving Wiley of all legal liability. My editor tore it up and said that if I was willing to do that, Wiley would stand behind me.

While all this was occurring, I kept locating information that had not been seen for a century or more. With the help of the likes of Jeff Morey, Gary Roberts, Jack Burrows, and Carl Chafin, I found a stunning amount of material. Imagine, sitting alone in a dark microfilm room and locating many articles that fill in critical details. It was quite an adventure.

EW: Let's talk about the O.K. Corral street fight. What was Wyatt's primary role in this affair and how did he reflect on this monumental event in his later years?

CT: In the fight itself, I think most historians now agree that Wyatt Earp fired the first shot almost at the same time as Billy Clanton fired, hitting Frank McLaury. Earp then fended off Ike Clanton, who raced forward to him then departed the scene as the Earp party focused its fire on Billy Clanton, Frank McLaury, and Tom McLaury. Through most of his life, Earp seemed to try and avoid discussing it. He believed he had done what needed to be done.

EW: Did Wyatt Earp kill John Ringo in the aftermath of Morgan's assassination in 1882?

CT: No. If Earp killed Ringo, he would have had to secretly return from Colorado to find Ringo in an obscure location, then shoot him down. If that happened, Earp never told the story to Lake, Forrestine Hooker, John Flood, or any of the other writers who tried to tell his story. It would be the most remarkable event of Earp's life, and he kept it a secret from his biographers. That seems unbelievable.

EW: After Tombstone, Wyatt and Josephine were somewhat nomadic. Describe their lives after Tombstone.

CT: Wyatt and their friends referred to Josephine as Sadie. They traveled the West, from boom to boom, searching for ways to make money. Saloons, horse racing, gambling halls. It was a life of adventure and opportunity. Earp ran saloons and invested in real estate in San Diego, he was involved in gambling operations in Seattle. He ran a stable in San Francisco, racing horses both in that city and on racetracks around the state. Sadie had a gambling problem that caused problems at times. They seemed to fight and resolve their differences. Sadie could make him laugh, which was what he liked most. In his later years, he settled into a mine on the California/Arizona border, where he would work during the winter, then spend the summers in Los Angeles or Oakland in rental houses or staying with the Welsh family. Always behind him was the specter of Tombstone, with magazines or newspapers dredging up the old stories.

EW: What was Wyatt like as an old man? Did he try to get his story told and if so, was he successful in his lifetime?

CT: I think — and this is opinion — that Prohibition was very good for Wyatt Earp. After being a heavy drinker for years, he seemed to spend the 1920s as a more sober senior citizen. Most of his summers were spent with the Welsh family in Los Angeles. Tina Welsh, who recently passed away, told stories of him walking her to the ice-cream store, then of serving him lunch in his final years. She said he was nice and polite. He still had the fire in him. He tried to sue after Walter Nobel Burns took his story without fair compensation.

After refusing to tell his version of events for years, Earp finally decided to talk. He was low on funds and wanted to leave something for Sadie. With the help of movie star William S. Hart, he proceeded to try and get his biography written, but there were many missteps. He finally connected with Stuart Lake, who could do the job. Unfortunately, Earp died before he could read the manuscript, and the book emerged containing many falsehoods.

Earp spent a good deal of time visiting the sets of the old silent western flickers and made a number of friends during his last years. It was an interesting end to a colorful life.

EW: You recently played a significant role as editor for the 2019 book *A Wyatt Earp Anthology: Long May His Story Be Told* (University of North Texas Press). Describe that project and what it has done for the field of Earp scholarship.

CT: Roy Young enlisted Gary Roberts and me to assist him in the *Anthology*. Gary and I thought it would probably take six to nine months. It wound up taking two-and-a-half years of full-time work. By the end, Roy was having vision problems and Gary was in the hospital. All and all, it was a monumental work and a tribute to the remarkable scholarship in this field. During the last quarter century researchers have dug out so much new information that has provided a much greater understanding of Earp and Tombstone. When we finished, we realized we could fill another anthology with the articles we had to leave out. Our hope was that the anthology would help set up the field for the next generation of writers. The study of Tombstone is of historical importance because the issues the townsmen faced in 1881 are not all that different from the issues we face today. Understanding the past can help wise folks shape the future.

Chuck Parsons is a former educator and school administrator who turned his attention to the history of the West many years ago. Since that time, Parsons has developed a reputation among both his peers and the reading public as one of the leading authorities on Texas history as well as outlaw/lawman history. He is the author of numerous books and was the recipient of the WWHA Best Book Award for *Captain John R. Hughes: Lone Star Ranger*.

EW (Erik Wright): The name "Chuck Parsons" is a pillar among western outlaw-lawman historians. How did you first become interested in the field of frontier history?

CP (Chuck Parsons): I guess when I was a kid, I got interested in frontier history by watching Saturday afternoon western movies; black and white motion pictures of course as that was before color TV. Somehow there was some advantage in identifying with the heroic action of those frontier characters. Do you remember when *Gunsmoke* was only on the radio? Before there was Matt Dillon to save Dodge City? I go back that far with the western and frontier characters.

EW: Considering your interest in the history of the West, what prompted you to tackle your first research project for publication?

CP: My first effort at writing something for publication was a lucky break indeed. On my first trip to Texas during the summer of 1976 I purposely met up with Barney Hubbs in Pecos, Texas. I had gotten familiar with him through my interest in Clay Allison, having read his booklet *Shadows Along the Pecos*. My intention was to drop in and say hello, basically. Fortunately, the drop in turned into a weeks-long effort. On meeting Mr. Hubbs in his office, he explained to me that his first edition was about sold out, yet he was having difficulty in finding the time to do another edition. He actually had the covers for it printed! What boiled down was that he was familiar with my writing "The Answer Man" column in *True West* magazine (then printed in Iola, Wisconsin with Jim Dullenty as editor) and he took a chance and asked if I would do the writing for the second edition. The deal was that I could use his office as a base, giving me the key to his office and stay as long as I liked. It was an ideal situation as I spent a week going through his files on Clay Allison. Went out through the day and had meals at the Pecos restaurant, spent my time writing on Clay Allison, protected every moment because Clay Allison's shotgun was behind the coach I used as a bed. After a week I felt I had done as much as I could, left the manuscript on his desk per our verbal agreement, and continued my Texas trip. So, you see – my first assignment was sheer luck. Who knows where I would be if I hadn't stopped in to say hello to Barney Hubbs?

EW: What lessons did you learn from that first publication about the research and writing process?

CP: Lessons learned? Actually, it wasn't an ideal research situation. Drilled into me was the fact that if you don't have access to the research materials you think you should have, then you are definitely limited. It's like trying to write about Tombstone, A.T. without the files of *The Nugget* or *The Epitaph*. Ideally you will have all your research materials together and then do the writing. The research of course is fun, but the writing is hard work. If you can keep everything in the proper chronological order then everything is fine, but sometimes getting your facts out of the right chronological order happens despite your best efforts.

EW: You have written about a variety of western characters from Phil Coe to Clay Allison to a host of Texas Rangers. Is there one that sticks out as a favorite? If so, why?

CP: Coe to Allison? Looking back, I would say the one that sticks out would be John Wesley Hardin and writing about his career and the many people connected with his life. Despite his many faults, he did have an impressive life: virtually all of Texas, Oklahoma Territory, Kansas cowtowns, a little into New Mexico Territory. But he had the fall-out of the Civil War, Reconstruction, the Texas State Police, had issues with the Texas Rangers and other lawmen, then Florida, then Huntsville State Prison, his pardon . . . thank goodness his letters were preserved and available to researchers as his photograph album . . . There is thus so much to deal with Hardin that you could spend your life and career making him the subject of your research – for a lifetime. And his relatives also make him an ideal figure for research: we should have a biography of the Clements brothers, his first cousins; of course, that brings in James Brown Miller and those guys . . . it's a huge proposition.

EW: What mentors did you have in the field when you began your career as a western historian?

CP: One of my early writers who was friendly and generous even if he wasn't an ideal historian was Carl W. Breihan of Missouri. He did do a lot of work with Jesse James and the Younger Brothers, which in the 1950s set a reasonable example. (I graduated from high school in 1958). But of real influence (mentors) I would say Ed

Bartholomew and C.L. Sonnichsen especially. They wrote about Texans and made efforts to be accurate. Of course, Phil Rasch and Fred Nolan were a big influence as well. We can't forget Joseph G. Rosa and Dale Schoenberger. Of course, what is "neat" is that although you admire their work in the field you can disagree and still be companions. They're all dead now, but their contributions live on, and they still have an impact on researchers and writers.

EW: Talk about life in Luling, Texas. Does small-town life make it easier to accomplish monumental writing tasks?

CP: Today living in Luling for me is an ideal spot. Maybe 6000 population; one grocery store which fills our needs. One bookstore in the entire county (which sells my books! *Aka* Mom's Front Porch) yet we are an hour from Austin with the Texas State Archives and the Briscoe Center for American History, and an hour from San Antonio with the 6th floor library and genealogy departments . . . for a retired couple we have easy access to what the big city has yet we have none of the headaches, such as traffic congestion.

EW: In your opinion why is Texas so good at maintaining a collective and protective interest in its history when many other states are beginning to forget or simply dismiss their own?

CP: We love our history because it is the best! We have our problems, what with some of the politicos trying to rewrite history and remove Confederate leaders . . . but that will someday change. We won't have the Left and Political Correction forever. Common sense will return!

EW: Overall, describe your research and writing methods.

CP: The only "method" is to tell the truth objectively. If you have an actual agenda keep it to yourself; save your personal feelings for the epilogue.

EW: As always, I like to close with parting advice for future historians. What nuggets of wisdom would you like to leave for the next generation of writers and researchers?

CP: Don't research and/or write about someone that you don't have a passion for. Other than the expected things, such as keeping events in chronological order and spelling correctly, have a passion for your subject – whether it be the Sand Creek Massacre or John Brown and Harper's Ferry. With a passion for your subject then find everything you can about him or her or the event and write accordingly.

David A. Wolff is a retired professor at Black Hills State University in Spearfish, South Dakota. He specializes in the history of the Black Hills, South Dakota, mining, and western history. Wolff's most recent book *The Savior of Deadwood: James K.P. Miller on the Gold Frontier* follows his biography of Deadwood lawman Seth Bullock and a study of Rocky Mountain coal mining.

EW (Erik Wright): Your new book *The Savior of Deadwood: James K.P. Miller on the Gold Frontier* (South Dakota Historical Society Press, 2021) sheds needed perspective on the Black Hills. Who was James K. P. Miller and what contributions did he make to Deadwood?

DAW (David A. Wolff): James K. P. Miller was a businessman, promoter, developer, and unsung hero of Deadwood. Miller arrived in the boomtown in early August 1876, just a few days after Wild Bill's killing. He did not come to pan gold or to join the card games. Instead, he came to "mine the miners." (As the old saying goes.) He and a partner set up a grocery store and exchange bank, known as Miller & McPherson's, on one of the camp's busiest corners. From the time they opened, Miller and his partner aggressively expanded their operations, and after a few years, they had the largest grocery business in the Black Hills, helping Deadwood become the region's service center. The fire that destroyed the town in September 1879, however, threatened Deadwood's preeminence. The gold rush had run its course and the hard rock mines sat three miles away. While the town was rebuilt, some people gave up on it, and a few pessimists predicted the end. Despite Miller's partner leaving, Miller stood fast. He had hope for the town, and he rebuilt his store.

But the former gold camp did not readily bounce back, and its population continued to drop into the 1880s. At this point, Miller took action to revive the economy. Working with a group of investors he called the Syndicate, he built a large building, known as the Syndicate Block in 1888. It would serve as the centerpiece of a renewed Deadwood. He and his investors also built the Deadwood Street Railway. As he saw it, all towns of any importance needed a street railway. Then to bring more business to town and to connect it with distant mining regions, he built the Deadwood Central Railroad, first to Lead and then beyond in 1889. Finally, he introduced smelting to Deadwood. He wanted the town to share in the mining economy, and he helped organize the Deadwood and

Delaware Smelting Company. Attracting an outside rail connection, however, sat at the heart of his vision for a thriving Deadwood. After many struggles, he finally convinced the Burlington and Missouri River Railroad to build in. It was followed in short order by the Fremont, Elkhorn & Missouri Valley Railroad. Because of these efforts, a newspaper reporter called him the "Savior of Deadwood." Sadly, Miller did not live to see the fruits of his labor. He died just as the railroads arrived, but his work endured, and Deadwood entered a new era of prosperity.

EW: Why are men like Miller not remembered today?

DAW: Some businessmen and developers endure in history because they ran large industries that changed the course of the American economy, such as Carnegie and Rockefeller. Others are remembered because they were scoundrels. Jay Gould comes to mind. George Hearst is remembered because of the vast scope of his mining empire (and perhaps because of the exploits of his son). Although critical for a town's survival, local developers, like Miller, are seldom remembered. When it comes to Western communities celebrating people, they focus much more on the infamous, such as the Wild Bills and Calamity Janes, in part because they draw tourists. Besides Wild Bill and Calamity Jane, Deadwood pays homage to businessmen W. E. Adams, Harris Franklin, and Seth Bullock. Certainly, they were important to Deadwood, but what helps them endure is that buildings survive with their names on them: The Adams Museum, the Adams House, the Franklin Hotel, and Bullock Hotel. All the buildings Miller had a hand in developing have disappeared. But fundamentally, what makes a Western personality last? He/she lived a life that was out-of-the norm, or on edge of legality, meaning it generally involved gunfights, which then became highlighted by dime novels.

EW: Talk about Deadwood in the era of Miller. What type of society did a boomtown create in the upper reaches of the Great Plains?

DAW: By the time Miller arrived, Deadwood was in full boomtown mode. Paying quantities of gold had been uncovered and it attracted more prospectors, as well as riffraff and camp followers, including Wild Bill and Calamity Jane. At this time, the nation was still suffering from the Panic of 1873, and some people saw easy money. Also, it had been a long time since there had been a gold rush, and gold camp veterans, especially those in Montana, wanted to come to Deadwood to try their luck. The paying quantities of gold also attracted middle class merchants, such as Bullock and Miller. While Main Street had an abundance of saloons and gaming halls, several reputable businesses opened. So, it was quite a heterogeneous mix of social classes and establishments. There were a few women, but most merchants, much like Bullock and Miller, left their wives behind and would only bring them to town after it had settled down. With prominent badlands and plenty of shady individuals, it is a wonder that a person like Miller survived and even prospered. But when he spoke about the situation, he just advised staying away from the bad places and mind your own business. It certainly worked for him. Interestingly, he ran a bank for three years and never once was he or it robbed.

While Deadwood celebrates 1876, the gold rush really peaked in 1877. Most, if not all, of the placer claims had been staked by 1877, but people kept coming, with

Deadwood's population reaching 6,000. Sadly, when the new arrivals could not find a claim or even work, they sometimes got lost in a saloon or gaming hall, until they figured out a way to get home. By 1878, the gold rush began to cool down and the general rowdiness had toned down. Bullock and Miller brought their wives by then, and "civil society" had taken root. Still, some gold town traditions continued, like the occasional outburst of violence. But by the 1880s, Deadwood resembled many other frontier towns in Dakota Territory.

EW: You have also written a biography of noted Deadwood lawman Seth Bullock. What is your assessment of Bullock as a peace officer?

DAW: Since Bullock was sheriff in Deadwood/Lawrence County for only about eight months, his record is a little sparse, but a few conclusions can be drawn. In the first place, I would call him "reactive." He didn't patrol the streets looking to stop trouble, he only responded when something happened, such as a shooting. Deadwood had a rather notorious badlands district, and Bullock never seemed to interfere. He did not arrest people for drunk and disorderly conduct, and when gunshots rang out, he only responded when they were done with malicious intent. Bullock's grandson once commented that when his grandfather hit Main Street at high noon, he wasn't looking for a shootout. Instead, he was looking for lunch. But when Bullock needed to display bravery, he did so without question. In at least two instances, he intervened in active shootouts, bringing them to an end without firing a shot himself. He seemed to have a forceful, no-nonsense personality that let people know who was in charge. On a more dubious note, Bullock and a deputy were once on a stakeout, hoping to capture a couple of alleged highwaymen. As the suspects approached, Bullock's weapon accidentally discharged. A few gunshots were then exchanged, but the forewarned men escaped. Bullock had never before participated in a shootout, and this might have been his one chance, but it all went wrong. By the time Bullock left the sheriff's office, he had not brought "law and order" to Deadwood, but he did establish some respect for the law. The voters of Lawrence County refused to re-elect him sheriff. It may have been that they resented the semblance of law that he brought. Or it could have been that his opponent, and eventual sheriff, ran saloons!

EW: How does the historic Bullock stack up against the character played by Timothy Olyphant in HBO's *Deadwood*? Would we remember Seth Bullock today if it was not for that series?

DW: I very much appreciated Timothy Olyphant's portrayal of Seth Bullock. He came across as the no nonsense kind of guy that Bullock was. Of course, the HBO show took a lot of liberties with Bullock. For instance, Bullock was fairly selective with whom he would associate. In fact, I think he saw himself a tad bit better than many other folks. Consequently, I doubt if he would have associated with Al Swearingen. Also, Bullock did not marry his brother's wife, as the show has him do. Instead, he married his childhood sweetheart, Martha.

Bullock certainly got national recognition because of the HBO show. One of the Discovery network channels did a "Gunslingers" series, and they included Bullock. I doubt if he would have been included had the HBO show not happened. He, however, would be remembered in Deadwood and South Dakota. People in this area recall him not only as the first sheriff, but he built a hotel and started the town of Belle Fourche. He also was a friend of Theodore Roosevelt. As a lasting tribute he had the Society of Black Hills Pioneer build a small tower a few miles outside of Deadwood right to honor Roosevelt right after his death. Now called the Friendship Tower, as people hike there, it reminds them of Roosevelt, Bullock, and their friendship.

EW: What inspires you as a historian?

DAW: I live in the Black Hills by choice. The Hills are my family home. I have two great-grandfathers buried near where I live. Consequently, I am inspired by these Hills, and then how humans have interacted with them. It is about human endeavor. When I was a youngster, I would kick around ghost town ruins and wonder what went on there. More tellingly, I would look at tumbled down mine buildings, which often contained old equipment, and wonder how it all worked and who was involved. That's how I got interested in James K. P. Miller. I became curious about the slag pile in lower Deadwood, and soon found out that Miller was the cause.

EW: What myths and misconceptions are there about Deadwood and the Black Hills that you would like to help clarify?

DAW: As with any "Wild West" town, plenty of myths and misconceptions exist, and thanks to social media repeating them, I am sure they will always be with us. Some of these myths have been around so long, they have become part of the Deadwood story. Instead of debunking them, I have discovered it to be more fruitful to explain how the myths started (if possible), and why they hang on. Nevertheless, here are a few myths and misconceptions that need to be mentioned.

First, how violent was Deadwood? If you believe the narrative behind the HBO show, there were two violent deaths a day. My work on Bullock told me that was wrong, but since then I have gathered a large amount of information on violence in Deadwood and the Black Hills. (Hopefully, it will be put into a book in the near future.) Nevertheless, I discovered that Deadwood was plenty violent, but not nearly the two deaths a day. There were times when there were violent outbursts, such as in August 1876, around when Wild Bill was killed. But that violence included intra-camp violence and Indian-white violence. If the violence is averaged out from Deadwood's beginning to the 1879 fire, it comes out to about one violent death every six weeks, and interestingly, not all of those killings happened in Deadwood proper. Some took place in nearby communities. While there was plenty of violence, it does not match the myth. I explore some of this in my Miller book.

Another HBO representation I get asked about is the language. I have read court transcripts where the participants quote what was said leading up to an event, and there was plenty of cussing. But generally, those people were doubting a person's parentage, meaning they used "bastard" and "s.o.b," but not the "f" word.

There are, of course, several stories associated with Bullock that are not true. One is that he was the first forest supervisor of the Black Hills. In reality, he was the second. Another is that he died in the Bullock Hotel. Instead, he died in his home in Deadwood's Ingleside subdivision. And there are others, but that is enough.

EW: What advice do you wish to leave with the next generation of western historians?

DAW: I am generally slim on advice but let me offer three thoughts.

1) Look at the landscape and question what you see. Much of the Black Hills landscape has been altered in some way. As you look at the landscape, wonder: what, why, who, and when.

2) Don't be afraid to ask small questions that seem only to deal with local topics. By exploring and answering several small questions, a larger understanding can result. I like to think of the Black Hills as a microcosm. (To use a term that has fallen out of favor) By figuring out what happened in this gold rush and boomtown environment, I can better understand what went on in other Western mineral fields.

3) Always research and write with a purpose, with a specific question in mind, and while doing so, ask yourself what new understanding or information can come out of it.

Dennis Larsen is a retired schoolteacher and current author and historian who has a passion for educating others. For years, Larsen has been captivated by early pioneer Ezra Meeker and his later quest to save the Oregon Trail from obscurity. Larsen has written extensively for many publications and is the author of three other books. He lives in Olympia, Washington.

EW (Erik Wright): Who was Ezra Meeker?

DL (Dennis Larsen): A very complicated man. People loved him or hated him. There wasn't a lot in between. He was incredibly stubborn and competitive. Once he chose a course, he was unmovable. He was generous to a fault, cared little about money and the trappings of wealth, was moral, but not particularly religious, and was a visionary. He could mix in seamlessly with governors and presidents as well as with the Native Americans who worked in his hop fields. He fought against the anti-Chines movement of the 1880s, backed the women's suffrage movement financially, and spent his money on projects that he felt would bring Washington Territory into the modern world.

EW: What attracted you to his story?

DL: On a road trip through the Blue Mountains in eastern Oregon we came across an Oregon Trail kiosk that briefly told his story. It mentioned that one of the stone monuments he placed in 1906 was nearby. While looking at it my wife said," I wonder where the rest of them are." Those words changed our lives. We went looking for them. Over the next two decades we learned his fascinating story, transcribed thousands of his letters, wrote four books and several articles about him, and lectured across the country about what he did during his 97 and 3/4ths years of life and followed both his and his partner's trail across the United States. (William Mardon was the partner.)

EW: Describe his first trek across the Oregon Trail when he was a young man. Was a typical experience of those who ventured across the Western trails?

DL: His crossing in 1852 was typical. Illness, dust, hardships galore, etc. His brother nearly died, and Ezra also fell ill for a time.

He was unusual in that he operated a ferry briefly at Council Bluffs and Fort Boise to earn cash, and no one in his group died. He did not keep a diary. The crossing of the continent, however, seared into his mind and 50 years later he could remember virtually every detail of the journey. He wrote extensively of it in his various books.

EW: What was life like on the West Coast for Meeker and the thousands of others who made the trip across the plains?

DL: Washington Territory was the end of the world for the pioneers of the 1850s. Settlements were few and small. Government was sketchy at best. San Francisco was its connection with the rest of the country. Almost all commerce went through that city. Besides farming, logging was the main enterprise. Its non-native population remained small until the coming of the railroads.

EW: In later years, Meeker became known as the "Hop King of the World." Can you describe what this means?

DL: In the 1860s Meeker began experimenting with hop growing. He eventually became the largest hop broker on the west coast and one of the larger growers in

Washington Territory. In the 1880s he pioneered the U.S. to London hop trade, and in the process became incredibly wealthy.

EW: At what point in Meeker's life did he begin to consider memorializing the Oregon Trail?

DL: In 1898 he joined the Klondike Gold Rush and wintered in Dawson City where he operated a grocery store. In a letter to his wife, he began a conversation about saving the memory of the pioneers. He came home in 1902 and over the next three years began working out his plan. In 1905 he went public with his plan.

EW: Talk about Meeker's preparation for his 1906 trip back to the Oregon Trail. Was there any significant public interest in his cause?

DL: His daughter was appalled at what her 75-year-old father was contemplating, a local minister told his congregation not to aid Meeker financially as "it would lead to the old man's death out on the plains." Nevertheless, he planned meticulously. He wrote dozens of letters to town leaders along his route, arranged in advance for lecture venues, contacted the local press and supplied them with photographs, built a covered wagon in part from a wagon that had crossed the plains in the 1850s, created a slide show to enhance his lecture, and arranged for a monument to be erected and dedicated at each of his stops. But he needed help. A drifter named William Mardon joined him at The Dalles, Oregon and stayed with him for the next six years and became an essential partner in the endeavor. Finances were always a problem. He wrote a book about what he was doing and sold 10,000 copies of it from Nebraska on. He also made hundreds of thousands of post cards of trail scenes that he also sold from his wagon. At many of the stops old pioneers stepped forward with meals and food and lodging for the oxen.

EW: Once Meeker set out on his quest back across the Oregon Trail did, he find that it was an easy trip? How had the landscape changed since he first visited the trail as a young man?

DL: It was anything but an easy trip. Two men with a forty some year age difference, with habits that at times grated, caring for and driving two oxen and a wagon from Seattle to Washington, DC. Camping out in the open air most nights and fighting financing for a good portion of the trip. The trail itself he found was fast disappearing to the plow and development. At times he had to solicit local help to locate what remained. Even the location of Fort Hall was lost to memory by 1906.

EW: In his lifetime do you believe Meeker was aware of his role as a sort-of living symbol for the transition of the frontier West into that of the urban West?

DL: He was very aware of it and often mentioned it to the local press at his stops. He felt, rightfully, that there was no one else among the old pioneers who were up to the task he had undertaken as they were dying off daily and he was in what he thought then was the twilight of his life. He never dreamed he would live another quarter of a century and carry on the fight till his last breath.

Jerry Enzler has spent his career enveloped in the history of the North American fur trade and westward expansion. Among his many honors and achievements include the 1979 opening if the Fred W. Woodward Riverboat Museum in Dubuque, Iowa as well as being awarded many grants for the restoration of structures associated with the history of the fur trade and westward expansion. He was written numerous museum exhibits as well as papers for the *Rocky Mountain Fur Trade Journal*, but his latest work, published by the University of Oklahoma Press explores the life of legendary mountain man in *Jim Bridger: Trailblazer of the American West*. Enzler is the Founder and President Emeritus of the National Mississippi River Museum & Aquarium, a Smithsonian Affiliate in Dubuque.

EW (Erik Wright): Who was Jim Bridger?

JE (Jerry Enzler): Jim Bridger was one of the most accomplished frontiersmen of the American West. His fifty-year career in the West spanned four distinct phases: exploration and the fur trade; the Oregon and California trail; guide for mapmakers and Smithsonian scientists; and chief guide to the U. S. Army during the Utah expedition and the Plains Indian wars. He rose to the top in each of these pursuits.

Bridger's founding of Fort Bridger and his role as scout and guide were as equally significant in U.S. history as were his fur trade days. He led topographers and scientists as they mapped and studied the west. He was chief guide to thousands of soldiers, finding grass and water for their horses, warning them of poisonous water holes and other dangers, stopping them from careless or overconfident behavior in Indian country, and keeping them alive.

Bridger almost single-handedly prevented a war with the Plains Indians. When gold was discovered in present-day Montana and Idaho, John Bozeman led the miners through lands claimed by the Lakotas, Cheyennes, and Arapahos. Knowing that this would lead to war, Bridger blazed a much safer trail in 1864 through Crow country. Oglala Lakota leader Red Cloud told the miners to take to Bridger Road instead of the Bozeman Trail. Neither the military nor the miners listened to Bridger and did not support the Bridger Trail. The result was three years of bloody conflict from 1865 to 1867.

As this book reveals, Jim Bridger was one of the original eight people proposed for the great monument in South Dakota. Once the sculptor was selected, the concept changed to memorialize four United States presidents.

EW: An iconic mountain man, where does a man like Bridger fit into the larger picture of the Rocky Mountain Fur Trade?

JE: Bridger went up the Missouri River when he was 18. At 21, he joined 26-year-old Thomas Fitzpatrick to lead a posse of older men to recover horses that had been stolen from them by the Bannock Indians.

When Bridger was 22, he was with William Sublette and several others who were the first known Euro-Americans to enter the present-day boundaries of Yellowstone National Park. At 26, Bridger, Fitzpatrick and three others formed the Rocky Mountain Fur Company.

Bridger soon knew more about the beaver country than anyone in the mountains. He was present at 14 of the 15-summer rendezvous and by the 1830s was considered the king of the mountain men. Even Hudson's Bay Company leader George Simpson tried to hire Bridger to join the British company.

EW: What set Bridger west across the Rocky Mountains at such a young age?

JE: Bridger was orphaned when he was 13 and he worked on a ferry boat across the Mississippi between the American Bottom in Illinois (where he lived) and St. Louis, Missouri. He apprenticed to Philip Creamer, one of the most celebrated gunsmiths in the United States. As told for the first time in this biography, twelve-year-old Jim Bridger and Philip Creamer lived adjacent to the Potawatomi Village on the Illinois river near Peoria, helping with repair of their guns, traps, and other metal tools.

At 18 Bridger was one of a hundred "Enterprising Young Men" who went up the Missouri River to trap beaver in Blackfeet country. He found his home in the Rockies and didn't come back to the settlements until 1839 when he was 35 years old. After a few months in St. Louis, Bridger turned west again and continued to live his life in the Rockies.

EW: What kind of life did men like Bridger live during his era?

JE: Bridger was equally happy leading a hundred trappers or riding alone to scout new lands or confirm the next day's journey for emigrants or soldiers. He made his home among the indigenous peoples, marrying a Flathead woman, and upon her death a Ute woman, and upon her death a Shoshone woman. He had seven children.

He could neither read nor write, but he carried a remarkable map of the West in his head and could recall the terrain ahead mile after mile. Bridger was exceptional, and people consistently remembered and wrote about the day that they met him. Bridger was one of America's great western heroes. Unlike Daniel Boone, David Crockett, and Kit Carson, Bridger did not have a historian, playwright, or journalist to write a full account of his adventures, but he was still known throughout the country.

Bridger was a fearless fighter when attacked by hostile forces, but he did not willfully attack adversaries. In 1838, Kit Carson, Joe Meek, Osborne Russell, and other free trappers attacked a Blackfeet village which was suffering from smallpox. Bridger argued against the attack and refused to participate or allow any of his hired man to join the assault.

Bridger guided many topographers and Smithsonian scientists including Howard Stansbury and John Gunnison in 1849-50, G. K. Warren and Ferdinand Hayden (who had discovered dinosaur fossils) in 1856, William Raynolds and Hayden in 1859-60, and Edmund Berthoud in 1861. They were all in awe of Bridger's skills. But both Stansbury and Raynolds doubted Bridger's advice though, and insisted on going their own faulty way, sometimes to serious consequences.

When guiding army troops during the Plains Indian wars, Bridger rose early almost every morning and had a quick cup of coffee and some jerked meat. He saddled up and rode to the commander's headquarters to go over the route for the day, the distance to the next camp, the contour of the route, and where to find good water and grass. Then he rode off alone to look for Indian sign, sometimes not returning until late. After giving the day's report, he cooked his frugal meal and found a place to sleep away from everyone else. While most army leaders valued Bridger's advice, some commanders also ignored his recommendations to their ultimate dismay.

EW: Was Bridger the young man (often identified as "Bridges") who, along with John Fitzgerald, abandoned Hugh Glass after his mauling by a mother grizzly bear?

JE: The jury is still out on whether Bridger was the youth who bravely volunteered to stay with Hugh Glass and was then persuaded by John Fitzgerald to abandon him in 1823. Moses "Black" Harris, Daniel Potts, and James Clyman all knew Bridger, and when they wrote of the Hugh Glass incident, they did not identify Bridger as the youth.

Then in 1839 an aspiring writer named Edmund Flagg wrote an error-filled story which said the youth was a 17-year-old named "Bridges." This new Bridger biography documents that there were several young men named Bridges who lived in Missouri in that era, so it could have been one of them. Or Flagg may have tried to insert Bridger's name because 19-year-old Bridger was the most famous of all the youth who were up the Missouri at that time.

This book brings to light perhaps the final word on the subject – Bridger's only comment about Hugh Glass. James Stevenson, a Smithsonian ethnologist who often "hunted and tented" with Bridger on scientific expeditions, said it was not Bridger. In response to an inquiry, Stevenson wrote from his office at the Smithsonian in 1886: "Bridger told me the story of your Glass; but there was no desertion [by Bridger]."

EW: Describe Bridger's life as an explorer and trailblazer.

JE: When Bridger was 20, he volunteered to follow the unknown course of the Bear River and became the first Euro-American to discover Great Salt Lake. When he was 21, he became the first person known to run the Bad Pass Rapids of the Bighorn River. He knew the Rockies so well that by the time he was 25, he was pilot for various brigades under company leaders Jedediah Smith, William Sublette, and David Jackson. He continued to explore new routes and cutoffs his entire life.

    The life of the Bridger and his companions is perhaps best described by Washington Irving who wrote: "A totally different class has now sprung up: 'the Mountaineers,' the traders and trappers that scale the vast mountain chains and pursue their hazardous vocations amidst their wild recesses. They move from place to place on horseback . . . hardy, lithe, vigorous, and active; extravagant in word, and thought, and deed; heedless of hardship; daring of danger; prodigal of the present, and thoughtless of the future. . . .. There is, perhaps, no class of men on the face of the earth . . . who lead a life of more continued exertion, peril, and excitement."

    Bridger loved to draw a new route in the dirt or on an animal skin. He was the primary resource for mapping the boundaries for the great Horse Creek Indian Treaty of 1851, and he also was the primary source for many maps drawn by Fr. Pierre De Smet, William Raynolds, William Collins, and others.

EW: What challenges did you encounter when researching and writing this book?

JE: My most significant challenge was that Bridger could not write, and he left very few letters behind, only those which he had dictated or asked others to write for him. I traveled to archives across the country and found letters, journals, and records of other people that told of Bridger's activities. I also searched through hundreds of books and articles which provided clues to where I could find more information about Bridger's life.

    A personal challenge for me was juggling this vitally important book with another project that also captured my energy. Just as I became interested in Jim Bridger, I had the good fortune to become the founder and Director of what became the National Mississippi River Museum & Aquarium, a Smithsonian affiliated, 14-acre museum campus. Because I was passionate about writing and storytelling, I was the leader for exhibit development, and I wrote and/or edited museum exhibits and films which have now been seen by over 4 million people. My museum work enabled me to meet and collaborate with archivists as well as nationally known historians and writers including Stephen Ambrose, John Barry, Edwin Bearrs, Doug Brinkley, Robert Utley, and many others who advised me on this Bridger biography.

EW: Are there still known Bridger descendants alive today?

JE: Yes. Bridger had seven children, and there are several Bridger descendants from his daughters Mary Elizabeth and Virginia. Bridger descendants meet every so often for family reunions at Fort Bridger and other locations.

Julia Bricklin is a noted historian has authored numerous books and dozens of articles on the female experience in the American West. Armed with a degree in journalism from Cal Poly San Luis Obispo, Bricklin worked for many years in Hollywood's television and film industry before earning a master's in history from Cal State Northridge. She is an associate editor of *California History* and a professor of history at Glendale Community College in Los Angeles.

EW (Erik Wright): Who Was Polly Pry?

JB (Julia Bricklin): "Polly Pry" was the nom–de–plume of Leonel Ross Campbell, journalist, and provocateur who lived in Denver in the late nineteenth and early twentieth century.

EW: How did Polly Pry emerge as a successful journalist in a world and era dominated by masculinity?

JB: Polly — Nell Campbell—saw how successful Nellie Bly (Nellie Cochrane Seaman, another female journalist) had been working for Joseph Pulitzer's *New York World*. Campbell recognized that owners of large newspaper companies wanted to take "yellow journalism" a step further and hire female reporters to lend an air of exoticism to their dailies. It had been successful in Pulitzer's east coast papers and William Randolph Hearst's west coast papers. Campbell knew there had to be a market for this in the non-coastal, Western states.

EW: What led you to the story of Polly Pry?

JB: I discovered Polly Pry quite by accident. I traveled to Denver in the hopes of writing a refreshed biography about Harry Heye Tammen and Frederick Gilmer Bonfils, the owners of the *Denver Post*. After half a day wading through their files at the Denver Public Library, I realized that I really could not add anything to Gene Fowler's *Timber Line,* or the wonderful retrospectives printed on occasion by the modern-day *Denver Post*. Some "Polly Pry" folders were mixed in with Tammen's and Bonfils'; once I started going through them, I was hooked. I knew I had to tell the real story of Nell Campbell.

EW: Regarding her frontier journalism, Pry is perhaps best known for her coverage of Tom Horn and Alfred Packer. How did Pry's work help to elevate the myth of these two notorious westerners?

JB: Superficially, of course, Pry's coverage of these two men (both convicted of murder—Packer of murder and cannibalism) after their initial convictions kept both of them in the public eye much longer. On a deeper level, though, Pry's coverage of Horn's trial and execution and her campaign to get Packer paroled gave readers a human angle to consider. For example, with Horn, she challenged her readers to ask, why would wealthy cattle barons put up $12,000 for his defense in the murder of 14-year-old Will Nickell? Yes, Horn was an irredeemable killer, but in this case, she maintained, he was a pawn for wealthy murderers who liked to keep their hands clean. And in Packer's case, through her writings, Pry showed the public that the purported cannibal was not an "inhuman beast" but rather, someone who was downtrodden by an unfair trial and a long incarceration. Polly Pry forced readers to consider Horn and Packer outside a vacuum—to consider the motives of others involved in their cases. I feel she elevated the myth of these two men by promoting vigorous discussion of the events and other people entangled in their lives.

EW: Following the closing of the frontier, Pry worked to champion a variety of humanitarian issues. Describe her efforts during this period.

JB: It might be a stretch to say Nell Campbell—Pry—championed a variety of humanitarian issues. She was not typical of the middle-class, Progressive Era woman. Through her writing, for example, she raised awareness of the plight of women and children who suffered from poverty during the "mining wars" of Telluride and Cripple Creek. But she did not necessarily work to raise money to alleviate their suffering. And certainly, she raised awareness of poverty in Mexican border towns, owing to warfare between that country and the United States—but she did not participate in any philanthropic efforts there. She was happy to leave that to other women and instead focus her efforts in a then-typically male arena: political fundraising and awareness. Only later in life did Polly Pry turn her attention to raising money for European children orphaned by conflict in World War I. When she did do this, she threw her heart and soul into it.

EW: Much of your published work in books and magazines focuses on the experience of women in the west. What challenges have you faced as a woman writing about women?

JB: I'm happy to say that I haven't faced any challenges as a woman writing about women! In fact, I never set out to write exclusively about my own gender. I look for great stories that haven't been told. I find that more often than not those stories are about women simply because historically female stories have been hidden behind those of men.

EW: Your next book, *Burmah Adams, Tom White, and the 1933 Crime Spree that Terrorized Los Angeles* is due to be released this summer. What drew you to this story of Depression-era Los Angeles?

JB: Just like "Polly Pry," I stumbled over Burmah's story by accident. I was looking for a photograph of an old-timey teacher for a fall issue of *California History*, a journal that I work for. A series of images popped up featuring Ms. Adams, because she and her husband had shot a schoolteacher in Los Angeles in 1933. Intrigued, I started wading through all of these trial photographs, and then I started researching the story. I'm thrilled that I have the chance to present this account of a young, beautiful, and smart woman who got caught up in a perfect storm of politics, corruption, Prohibition, and love.

Elliott West, a professor of history at the University of Arkansas and longtime historian of Westward expansion gained recognition in the field with such works as *The Contested Plains: Indians, Goldseekers, and the Rush to Colorado* among others. He is the winner of the 1999 Francis Parkman Prize, a co-winner of the Ray Allen Billington Prize, a two-time recipient of the Western Heritage Award, and the past president of the Western History Association.

EW (Erik Wright): Your new book *Continental Reckoning: The American West in the Age of Expansion* seems to have been an incredible undertaking. Can you describe how the project came to be?

West (Elliott West): I've studied and taught western American history for quite a while—more than fifty years. I love all of it, but the part that most interests me is when that stretch of country from the Missouri River to the Pacific came into being as what we call today "the West." The birth of the West, I suppose. It starts when we added well more than a million square miles between 1845 and 1848 and pushed the nation fully across the continent. By around 1880, in only about a generation, the West had pretty much come into focus. It's during that time that so many of the events that most folks identify with the West took place—the great overland migrations, gold and silver rushes, Indian wars, the transcontinental railroad, homesteading, plains ranching, explorations, and so much more. It is such a fascinating and mythic time in our history. It long ago grabbed me and it has never let me loose.

    So, when Dick Etulain and the University of Nebraska Press asked me to write its history as part of their series, I quickly said "yes." The more I pursued it—and it's been more than twenty years since I took it on—the more a couple of things became clear. First, there was so much more to the story than I had anticipated. I became much caught up, for instance, in how the West in these years was one of the world's most active and productive scientific laboratories, with fundamental breakthroughs in so many fields, from geology and paleontology to the study of diseases and the weather. Second, it became ever clearer that I was really working with two stories. The birth of the West was plenty interesting and important in its own right, but it was also absolutely crucial to the larger one of the birth of modern America—the changes the nation went through during those same years that made us into the nation and people we would know in the 20th and 21st centuries. I came to think that my job was to tell something of how the two fit together and, taken together, how they can help us understand who we are today.

Those are both big stories, and I was determined to give them a human dimension, what I call a sense of "sombodyness." Over the years I have worked to collect as much as I can of the voices of ordinary folks as they lived through that extraordinary time. In this book I have tried hard to include their stories and their voices. That has been especially fun.

EW: How does this book stand alongside or complement other sweeping histories of the American frontier experience like Richard White's *A Republic for Which it Stands* and Frederick Merk's *History of the Westward Movement*?

West: Richard of course writes on a far larger canvas, telling the story of Gilded Age America (and doing it brilliantly, I think). As a Western historian he does bring much of the West in and works, as I do, to place it in the narrative of the emergence of modern America. He even has a chapter entitled "Greater Reconstruction," a term I coined, which integrates the evolving West after the Civil War into this crucial and much misunderstood era. Merk's much earlier classic is a history not of the West as I treat it, as a region, but of the westward *movement*, that is, the frontier. His West is a moving target. Mine stays put, as a place, but its changes were enormous.

EW: Is it fair to assume that not everything can be included in a book despite its size and historical coverage? How do you begin to narrow the focus of this broad and often complex story of westward expansion while still driving a readable narrative?

West: That was really the biggest challenge of writing the book. The problem was not only what to include and what to leave out—you're right of course; it's impossible to even touch lightly on everything—but also how to put it all together, how to come up with a structure that makes sense and fits together reasonably well. Some big topics have a natural structure. I am one of many who think of the Civil War as a perfect Elizabethan drama in five acts. The Western story is the opposite. So much in so many areas happened so fast with so many overlapping, interrelating consequences. It's all energy and movement and rapid change. It makes me think of the familiar line of the Canadian humorist Stephen Leacock who wrote of a character who "flung himself upon his horse and rode madly off in all directions."

My choice was to divide the book into three parts. The first, "Unsettling America," covers from expansion and the simultaneous discovery of gold in California to the end of the Civil War. Its themes are uncertainties, violence, government floundering. Expansion was supposed to lead to a new era of national greatness. Instead, it nearly destroyed the republic. As the East was splitting art, the West often seemed about to fly apart. The second part, "Things Come Together," follows the consolidation of the West, the building of an infrastructure of rails and roads and wires, the role of the West in science, including consigning Indians to a lower level of civilization, and a pause to look at the human composition of the new West—at just who was there. Part three, "Worked Into Being," follows three familiar developments, the rise of ranching, of a spreading agriculture, and of mining, but I try to paint them in a new and more revealing light. I also take the Native story, which weaves through everything earlier, and follow it to its end, including their resilience, persistence, and adaptation. It's a tall order, trying to keep all of this together, and I hope it works.

EW: Let's talk about you, the man who became this historian. What first sparked your interest in history and specifically Western history?

West: Becoming a western historian was accidental. I grew up in a newspaper family but always was strongly drawn to history. My father used to say that journalism was just history in a hurry. He was an editor and my brother a successful travel journalist. I majored in journalism and was ready to head into that world, but on a whim, I applied to the graduate program in history at the University of Colorado. I liked history, and I liked Colorado. What could be more obvious? I was stunned when, first, I was accepted with a very plush three-year fellowship and, second, when I got to Boulder and learned that I was supposed to specialize in something. I had no idea of what to say. (I blurted out antebellum southern history, but they said they didn't do that.) I had not the slightest clue that their strength was in western history, but I took Bob Athearn's seminar that first fall, and that was it. I've been in love with the West and its story ever since.

EW: When did you know that you wanted to follow a career in academia?

West: Well, I had greatly admired my best teachers, both during college and before, and I think occasionally I had thought something along the lines of "Gosh, maybe I could do that," and I had come to envy their chance to pursue an intriguing research a topic in depth (Remember: journalism is history in a hurry), but until that invitation to grad school in Colorado I had not thought of either as a possibility. Only in Boulder did I get a taste of what that life is like. As I said, I was infinitely naïve about what to expect, so looking back it was all a continuing stroke of the best luck, for which I am beyond grateful to whatever gods allowed it all to happen.

EW: Your book, *The Contested Plains,* is considered by many to be one of the great classics of Western historical writing written in the 20th-century. Can you talk about that book some?

West: This also goes back to Colorado. I grew up in Texas, and like so many Texans we would run away to Colorado in the summers. My grandmother owned a house in Georgetown, Colorado, and I came to not only love the state but also to be fascinated with its story, especially that of mining towns. My first book was on that (specifically saloons and what they teach us about community). I decided to write a social history of the Colorado gold rush. Then I used a year-long fellowship to the Newberry Library to retool my interests from social to environmental history, which others like Bill Cronon, Don Worster, and Richard White were practicing so brilliantly), and it dawned on me that the story of the rush on the plains was at least as revealing as that in the mountains. Specifically, the story was a universal one—the continuous conversation among people, the land, and all of life on (and under) it. The rush on the central plains, once we look at it as part of "deep history" of the centuries before it and a story involving all actors, certainly including Native peoples, was something close to a perfect case study of that and one that I thought could help us understand generally the history of the West during those years. I learned a hell of a lot.

EW: You have the benefit of perspective from seeing the field of Western history and its historians evolve from the 1960s through today. What significant changes have you seen in this time and what do you think the future of the field is in the coming decades?

West: The first question is a lot easier to answer than the second. Most obviously the perspective has broadened enormously—women's history, history of various ethnic peoples, including Native groups, environmental history, the history of frontiers newly defined, the revival and enrichment of borderlands history, history with international borders more permeable or entirely erased, and a lot more. Compared to the ones I knew when I first attended, the annual program of the Western History Association seems to be from another planet. I think that is overwhelmingly for the good. There is such a vitalizing infusion of young blood and young ideas in our field. It's exhilarating. Like other old duffers in the guild, however, I miss the more traditional topics and their advocates, the "buffs" who are largely absent from our gathering. One of the strengths of western history, compared to other areas of American history, has been its broad and welcoming appeal outside academia. I think we need to work more toward shoring that up. I think also some new scholars could work more on communicating their ideas more clearly and accessibly. Maybe they ought to take a few courses in journalism.

As for the second question, like many others I have come to see that historians are perhaps the worst predictors in our society. We're really hopeless. That said, working on *Continental Reckoning* has made me aware of some areas that we might pursue freshly. As I mentioned above, I think the work of science in the West is greatly underappreciated and understudied. It's quite a story. And religion, not the history of denominations in the West—we have plenty of those—but rather the role of religion in everyday lives, including those of Native peoples and how religion of Native and newcomers interacted. Beyond that your guess is as good, or as bad, as mine.

EW: I often like to close these interviews with the opportunity for the historian to offer advice for younger generations of researchers and historians emerging in the field. What are your primary pieces of wisdom in this regard?

West: I just mentioned my unsolicited advice of trying to communicate more clearly and to appeal to a broader audience. Beyond that: follow your nose and your curiosity, engage your peers and your elders, and argue with them, read, read, read, accept that for all its simplistic image western history is profoundly complicated and of many, many voices, don't be afraid make your history funny when it says it is. Keep the faith in pursuing what I like to think of the The Great Chase.

James B. Mills is based in New South Wales, author and historian James B. Mills has had a longtime interest in the history of the American frontier. His work has previously appeared in *True West* and *Wild West* magazines, *The Tombstone Epitaph*, and his new book, *Billy the Kid: El Bandido Simpático*, was recently released by the University of North Texas Press to high acclaim including a Will Rogers Gold Medallion.

EW (Erik Wright): *Who was Billy the Kid in myth versus reality?*

JBM (James B. Mills): In myth, he was a larger-than-life demonic caricature who constantly went looking for trouble, relished becoming a famous outlaw, and would coldly shoot a man down out of pure malice. In reality, he was an impish, scrawny, orphaned Irish teenager making his way through a harsh and violent time and place, who tried repeatedly to get out of the outlaw life, was remarkably well-liked by the vast majority of those who knew him personally, and didn't care much at all for the fame he was bestowed. He was no saint of course. He was a brazen thief at times and shot his share of men on the southwestern frontier, but he clearly wasn't a malicious sociopath either. Even Pat Garrett defended his character. To be honest, I don't have much time for Billy the Kid; he's mostly myth. Henry McCarty, alias William H. Bonney, is a lot more interesting.

EW: Describe your interest in Billy the Kid. How did a thirty-something Australian pick up a fascination with an American outlaw?

JBM: I was instinctively drawn to history for as long as I can remember. Even in kindergarten, I held a fascination for cowboys, Indians, pirates, and knights. What really fueled my passion for frontier history was watching old-time westerns with my mother on the weekends when I was a youngster. While other little kids were reading Goosebumps books, I was reading about Sitting Bull. I had heard of Billy the Kid, but it really started one night when I was flipping through the TV channels on my couch when I was nine years old. I can still remember that fateful night as clear as day. I was channel surfing, when suddenly, some handsome young fellow with a hyena laugh spat on some big guy's head from a rooftop on my television screen. It was Emilio Estevez in Young Guns II. I thought that was really funny. I watched the rest of movie, hit the video store soon after to rent both films and I was hooked. That was how I was bitten by the Billy-bug. I started reading whatever I could find about him, although living in Australia, I didn't have a wide variety of materials available to me back then. As the years passed, I found the historical reality far more interesting than the movie depictions, as is often the case. I'll always have a soft spot for Estevez and screenwriter Jon Fusco though. Without them, I might not be the historian I am today, and my book may not have been written.

EW: Your new book *Billy the Kid: El Bandido Simpático* is the first book to fully explore the relationship between the Kid and his Hispanic friends. Describe those relationships and why they are important to the Kid's story.

JBM: He was as much "Beely" as he was Billy—more so even. As one of his many amigos Apolicarpio "Paco" Anaya later said, "Billy liked better to be with Hispanics than with Americans." Truth be told, a book like mine should have been written decades ago. My dear friend Lynda A. Sánchez was planning to do so back in the 1980s but got sidetracked with other subjects. She has been one of my book's biggest champions. The Hispanos were the people whom Billy lived amongst and arguably knew him best. He adapted to their culture, which was vastly different from his own in many ways and crossed the cultural divide to a greater extent than most Anglos did in his time. It is clear that he mostly preferred their company to his fellow Anglos, and he treated them with immense kindness and respect. He was a demon of the Anglo press, but a champion of la gente. To most of the Hispanos of his time, Billy was a true friend and a hero—whether some people can accept that or not. I prefer to write about flesh and blood human beings and leave the heroes and villains stuff to Marvel movies, but Billy did enjoy a remarkably simpático relationship with the Hispanos of south-eastern Nuevo México.

I wish I knew the reason why the Hispano side of Billy's history and their perspectives have been routinely dismissed by various historians. There have been instances when first-hand Hispano recollections of events have been disregarded in favor of second-hand Anglo hearsay, which is inexcusable. William Keleher was one of my favorite historians, but that he only mentioned Martín Chávez once in the footnotes of his hefty Violence in Lincoln County 1869-1881, despite Martín having been the appointed leader of the McSween partisans during the five-day siege in Lincoln and such a close friend of the Kid, is truly baffling. In writing my book, well, if you write a biography of any famous person, even an actor or a musician, which sources would you put more stock in; the recollections and feelings of the people who actually knew and spent the most time around the individual, or what the tabloids and gossip magazines wrote about the person? For me, the answer is a no-brainer, and I afforded Bonney that one courtesy.

EW: Is Billy the Kid remembered differently in the Hispanic circles of the borderlands than he is by others?

JBM: I don't want to speak on behalf of modern-day Mexican Americans of the borderlands. I don't feel I have the right to do that, nor do they need me to try to act as a spokesman for them. Their history has often been distorted by gringos enough. I will say that the Hispanos of Billy's time cherished his memory long after his death. Many went to their graves defending his character and legacy decades after the American Frontier had faded into history. Their perspective and warm feelings for him were often passed down through the generations of course. Modern-day Native New Mexican author Denise Chávez once said it best; "New Mexicans felt that he was one of us." I think anyone who reads my book will probably get away from it with similar feelings. He was definitely their Billy more than anyone else's.

EW: Your book tackles the question of Billy the Kid's origins and offers one enticing possibility discovered by historian Jack DeMattos. Will we ever truly know the facts about the earliest years of Billy the Kid or his ancestors?

JBM: It's possible, but I wouldn't bet much on it. He was in all probability born in New York in around 1859-1860. I think Jack DeMattos has come closer than any of us and probably has it right. Unfortunately, without something that irrefutably links the Catherine, Henry, and Joseph McCarty of his findings to the ones who were standing with William Antrim in the First Presbyterian Church on the corner of Grant and Griffin Streets in Santa Fe on March 1, 1873, I couldn't write of his findings as definitive. I hope Jack understands that. There's been 101 theories about the Kid's origins, none of which led to anything definitive. Sometimes historians just need to admit when we simply don't know the answer, rather than further muddying the historical waters with theories that lead nowhere.

EW: Describe your research and writing process. What challenges did you face in the development of this book while living on the other side of the globe? How did your mentors aid in your maturity as a writer and researcher?

JBM: The challenges were lessened greatly with the generosity and assistance of various historian friends and some wonderful archivists over there. Chuck Usmar and Lynda A. Sánchez went above and beyond in supporting my ambitions and championing my work. The late Bob Utley kindly sent me his digitized research notes. Bob Boze Bell and Richard W. Etulain both endorsed me and offered advice. My writing style is entirely mine and purely instinctive, but I took on valuable pieces of advice from those with more experience and it made me a better writer. My writing often has a smooth narrative style, but strictly based on hard-nosed historiography. I never create dialogue for which there is no historical record. It irritates me when some people simply parrot the narratives of previous authors without looking at the original sources of information, doing any original research, and trying to dig deeper. If you are just going to write the same old kind of book about Wild Bill Hickok, Wyatt Earp, or Billy Bonney without bringing anything new to the table, then what's the point? I guess some people are more interested in simply making money than the actual advancement of history.

EW: In your book, you write that, "Historically, William Bonney towers over every one of the Territorial power players with whom he had some degree of conflict..." What sets Billy the Kid apart from his contemporaries in this regard?

JBM: He had far more personality and charisma. In many cases, he was also a lot more likeable and relatable too, horse and cattle thief though he was. There is some irony in the fact that men like John Chisum and Charlie Goodnight stole more livestock than Billy Bonney probably ever looked at. The Kid's story made for a broader and more engaging story, and he was also gifted the most memorable alias of any outlaw in frontier history by the press. Although, he wasn't the only person referred to as "Billy the Kid" on the southwestern frontier. Billy Claibourne was also given that handle in Arizona. At the end of the day, I guess there was only room for one legend in the annals of New Mexico banditry. There's a reason there have been over sixty films made about him; he's the biggest box-office attraction in New Mexico history, regardless of how one feels about his exploits.

EW: Many historians, including the late Robert Utley, make comparisons between Billy the Kid and Australia's Ned Kelly. How did these outlaws or social bandits become legendary folk heroes?

JBM: Personally, I'm not a fan of comparisons. Billy Bonney was Billy Bonney, Ned Kelly was Ned Kelly, John Dillinger was John Dillinger, and so on. For an outlaw to become a folk hero, they need to have possessed some semblance of a cause. Having a charming and affable personality also helps. There have actually been far more outlaws and criminals who didn't become folk heroes than those who have. There are levels to everything, even outlawry. No outlaw who raped women or murdered innocent people out of pure sadism is going to become a folk hero, at least not to any sane person. There have been exceptions—I can't understand the romanticization of a couple of genuine psychopaths like Bonnie and Clyde—but social bandits are pretty rare in the grand scheme of things.

In Billy's case, he was already a folk hero among the Hispanos at the time of his own death. Although the newspapers were embellishing his activities and portraying him as the worst person imaginable, given the majority Hispano population at the time, Billy probably had far more supporters than detractors in south-eastern New Mexico when he was killed by Pat Garrett. Sensationalist writers like Walter Noble Burns came along decades later and helped popularize the legend, like Stuart Lake did for Wyatt Earp. A social bandit provides us with that likeable rogue that appeals to many in society, especially younger and rebellious-minded people. It's the same with some rock stars and Hip-hop artists. The same reason a thieving, charming scallywag like Captain Jack Sparrow became one of the most popular film characters of the last twenty years. To quote the late Hunter S. Thompson, "In a nation of frightened dullards, there's always a sorry shortage of outlaws, and those few who make the grade are always welcome." Can you hear that? It's the sound of another self-appointed moral preacher about to climb aboard his or her own personal soapbox and throw another selectively outraged hissy fit when reading this. You can tell those snobs in Santa Fe who don't consider Billy the Kid to be "historically worthy," that I do not have their best interests in mind.

EW: If presented with the opportunity what one question would you ask Billy the Kid?

JBM: That's easy; "Okay Kid, exactly when and where in the hell where you born?" Bonney didn't believe in letting the truth get in the way of a good story, but hopefully he'd shoot me straight on that.

Jean Johnson has spent decades researching the history of one of America's least understood regions: Death Valley. She is the author of several books, magazine and journal articles, and served on the board of directors of the Death Valley '49ers, Inc. Johnson's latest book, *Grit and Gold: The Death Valley Jayhawkers of 1849*, tells the true story of a group of young men who faced insurmountable challenges in the desert as they traveled west to seek their fortunes in the California gold fields.

EW (Erik Wright): Who were the Death Valley Jayhawkers?

JJ (Jean Johnson): The Jayhawkers were about two dozen, mostly young men, from Western Illinois who were heading for the California gold fields in spring 1849. They held initiation rites along the Platte River, and when, with a number of other emigrants, they became lost in the mountains and deserts of Nevada, they ultimately blundered into Death Valley. Their number increased during their arduous escape through the California deserts, and they have since been called the Death Valley Jayhawkers.

EW: As a place, how did Death Valley impact the bodies and minds of those seeking their fortunes in California?

JJ: Death Valley was just one of many desolate desert valleys with bad water, but this one was so rugged, they could not get their wagons across where they entered the valley. They abandoned their wagons and carts just south of the sand dunes and walked across 250 miles of sand and gravel to a Mexican Rancho in southern California. As food became scarce, the thought "when will this end," must have occurred often. They had no concept of the expanse of the western landscape. It was daunting. Their lips cracked, their tongues swelled, their boots wore out, and their bodies were reduced literally to skin and bones. When they got to the top of the Panamint Range on the west side of Death Valley, they were sure they would be able to see the Pacific Ocean. Imagine their consternation and dread when they saw the mighty Sierra Nevada still 50 miles to the west.

EW: How did Death Valley get its name?

JJ: Death Valley was named by one of the '49ers who turned south in Death Valley. Captain Richard Culverwell, an older man, died near a small water well south of today's Bennett's Well. His body was found by Lewis Manly and John Rogers when they returned with food to rescue the Bennett and Arcan families waiting in Death Valley. On the families' way out to civilization, W. Lewis Manly, Asahel Bennett, and John B. Arcan, climbed to the crest of the Panamints where they looked back over the salty valley, removed their hats, and said "Goodbye Death Valley." We think it was Lewis Manly who named the valley: The words of farewell were spoken on February 13, 1850.

EW: The Donner Party may be more remembered for their suffering in the Sierras during the winter months of 1846-1847, but how do the Jayhawkers of 1849 fit into the larger context of Western history and the idea of Manifest Destiny?

JJ: Manifest Destiny expressed the assumption that expansion of Eastern US culture was inevitable and just. The Jayhawkers were not interested in expanding into the west; they were going for adventure and to seek their fortune. Some succeeded and returned home, but others became part of Manifest Destiny when they settled in California and became solid citizens. They became farmers, ranchers, businessmen, miners, and some have family relatives who still live in California.

EW: How did the 1849 Jayhawkers survive such a harsh environment?

JJ: The short answer is: They supported one another! Their feet were callused and toughened. They grew beards to protect their faces from the sun. They had already walked almost 2000 miles and were used to camping out. They had already experienced dust storms, sunburn, diarrhea, freezing nights, burned bread, and thirst. They learned to put one foot before the other as flies sucked blood from their cracked lips. They singed the hair off ox hide and ate it; they squeezed the offal out of ox intestines and fried them. They draped a fellow Jayhawker on the back of an emaciated ox instead of leaving him to die, they trudged miles to take water to their comrades.

EW: The story of the Death Valley Jayhawkers is well over a century old and covers numerous states. What challenges did you face during your research for *Grit and Gold*?

JJ: The migration trails from Illinois to Salt Lake have been well researched. The Nevada/California mountains and deserts, however, require closer attention. Diaries and later writings of the '49ers were essential; then fitting those descriptions to the terrain was required. A lot of desert canyons look alike. Therefore, my husband LeRoy (and I) had to hike all plausible ones to see which fit the '49er's descriptions best, often going back numerous times. Maps can actually be misleading. You have to see the desert terrain as the '49ers saw it, you have to consider their needs for water and forage for the oxen, to consider their goal of finding Walker Pass through the Sierra Nevada.

EW: What became of the men following their ordeal in the desert?

JJ: Those who survived made their way up the coast to the gold camps and worked the river gravels from Merced north to the Feather River. Some returned home within a few months having found enough gold to satisfy their needs. A few may have thrown up their hands and said, I'm out of here! Several kept trying to make their fortune for several years before going back East. Others decided to settle in the new state and take up farming, ranching, or hauling as they had in Illinois. A few were miners for the rest of their lives. Most married and reared children.

EW: You have written extensively about the history of Death Valley in a number of books, magazines, and journals. What should *Epitaph* readers know about the history of the region and how it helped to shape the frontier west?

JJ: By knowing the human history—from the Indians, mountain men, pioneers, settlers, to more recent development—one gains an additional dimension to appreciate the desert Southwest. Fortunately, much of the desert land traveled by the '49ers are still sparsely settled. Step away from the asphalt, walk into the scrub and rocks and gravel, listen to the wind. When you are comfortable with it, you find an inner strength that is hard to describe. That inner confidence, the feeling that "I can do it" is, to me, the core attribute that shaped the frontier west. By reading about the grit, gumption, humor, and loyalty to friends the Jayhawkers exhibited, each one of us can be proud of those who came before us and at the same time, use them as a standard to give more backbone to our own lives. We can transfer their gumption to our own attitude that "I can do it."

John Boessenecker is one of the most respected Western historians writing today and has turned his attention to California's famous, but elusive Black Bart in a groundbreaking new book which seeks to tell the whole story of the bandit's life. His other works include biographies on noted Pima County (Arizona Territory) Sheriff Bob Paul, outlaw Bill Miner, outlaw Pearl Hart, legendary California Tiburcio Vásquez, and many others.

EW (Erik Wright): Let's talk about your newest book *Gentleman Bandit: The True Story of Black Bart, the Old West's Most Infamous Stagecoach Robber.* What sparked your interest enough in this story to write a full-length biography of Black Bart?

JB (John Boessenecker): I first read about Black Bart (true name Charles E. Boles) when I was a teenager. Since then, I have collected information, documents, and photographs related to his story. In the early 1990s three excellent books about him were published; I assisted the authors of two of them. Each of those books contains much research that does not appear in the others. I decided to combine the information in those three books, as well as my own research, into a full-length biography.

EW: It may come as a surprise to some readers but relative to other famous Westerners, Black Bart has not had much written about him over the years. Why do you think this is?

JB: The main reason is that he covered his tracks so well. He was hard to catch; it took the best lawmen in California eight years to track him down. Then it has taken historians another 140 years to track down his real story -- his family history, his early life, his valiant army service in the Civil War, his letters to his wife and daughter. Another problem has been the huge number of myths that sprang up over the years, for those have obscured the facts of his life and career as a stage robber.

EW: How did the crimes of Black Bart impact the policies of Wells Fargo?

JB: Black Bart was just one thorn in the side of Wells Fargo. The company had to deal with hundreds of stagecoach and train robbers. In response, Wells Fargo employed a cadre of crack express detectives led by the brilliant James B. Hume. As pioneers in American policing, they developed every skill imaginable: using photographs for identification of suspects, quick communication by telegraph, primitive forensics, and employing local scouts and manhunters to track down bandits in frontier regions.

EW: What about those of the police in California and elsewhere?

JB: In the frontier era, police and sheriffs developed at highly different rates. Many rural sheriffs and city marshals, due to the bitter and divisive politics of that era, were voted out of office every two to four years. That prevented many of them from obtaining experience. Some police and sheriff's departments were removed from politics and became extremely well managed, professional, and effective. A good example is San Francisco, which was one of the finest law enforcement agencies in the American West. But at the same time, Black Bart lived quietly in San Francisco, posing as a wealthy mining investor, and he became good friends with some of its best police detectives, including Ed Byram and Chris Cox. They had no idea that their companion -- a jolly, well-traveled, former U.S. army officer -- was America's most notorious stage robber.

EW: Much of Black Bart's life remains a mystery. Were you able to flesh out some of these unknown details in your new book?

JB: Yes, and that was a major motivation in writing the book. I quote from numerous letters he wrote to his wife and daughters, and I even have a photo of them, taken in the 1880s, that has never been published before. I have three detailed chapters on his Civil War career; his experiences help explain his later career as a bandit. I also lay to rest many of the wild yarns and myths: that he ended up in Japan or Australia; that he robbed with an unloaded shotgun; that Wells Fargo cheated him out of his mine in Montana; that he is buried in Marysville, California. In doing my research, I visited the scenes of many of his stage holdups and even the house his wife and daughters occupied in Hannibal, Missouri.

EW: Where does someone like Black Bart fit into the larger tapestry of California history? How is he remembered there today?

JB: To this day Black Bart is recalled as one of the most colorful characters of Old California. There are still Black Bart festivals; numerous streets and roads are named after Black Bart; his hideouts (some real, some not) are routinely marked for tourists to see. And the shotgun that he used in his last stage holdup is in the collection of the Gene Autry Museum in Los Angeles.

EW: Was stagecoach robbery big business in the Old West or did characters like Black Bart steal the headlines therefore making it seem like the problem was worse than it really was?

JB: Stage robbery was a big problem in the Old West. Stages carrying Wells Fargo shipments were held up more than 340 times between 1870 and 1884. That does not include coaches that did not carry Wells Fargo's treasure. The first stage robbery in California took place in 1856; the last holdup of a horse drawn stage in the West took place at Jarbidge, Nevada, in 1916. During those sixty years I would estimate that at least a thousand stages were robbed.

EW: You write about a wide variety of outlaws and lawmen from all across the West. What is next for you and why did you choose that subject?

JB: My current book project is a biography of Joaquin Murrieta, the most famous Latino outlaw of the Old West. People have been asking me for many years to write a book about him, but I have always shied away from that because 90% of what has been written about him is myth and fiction. Trying to weed through all that -- to separate the myth from the fact -- would be a monumental effort. Instead, my book will concentrate on primary sources and thus avoid all the wild yarns and legends. That way I hope to provide the most accurate account of Joaquin's bloody career.

Kurt House is a sort-of renaissance man in the field of Western history. He has previously published six books on everything from archaeology to antique firearms to natural history to spurs. He is also a noted historian of the southwest and co-authored *Chasing Billy the Kid* with fellow historian Roy B. Young.

EW (Erik Wright): Kurt, you are known widely as a collector and appraiser of Western antiques and firearms. How did you become interested in that hobby?

KH (Kurt House): Well, Erik, I suppose I was originally inspired by my father, a WWII Battle of the Bulge veteran who was a collector himself, having brought back some souvenirs from the war, but also, I received a respect for history from both grandfathers. Some psychologists insist that collectors are made, while others contend that collectors are just born that way. I am not sure which category I fall into, but I feel blessed that my ancestors imparted to me a respect and admiration of the western lifestyle because I grew up on a Texas ranch.

EW: How do collectors protect themselves from fraudulent items in the Western antiques market?

KH: I am glad you asked this question, about fakery in the antiques business, because it has become rampant in the past couple of decades due to the enormous increase in value of some collectibles. You can predict what fakers will fake, because as soon as something becomes worth faking, they do it. Nowadays, no collector or collection is immune, because none of us can be experts in all areas; personally, I collect antique arms, photography, books, spurs, and other cowboy equipment and despite a lifetime spent in study, I still learn every day. A collector who ceases to learn is a fool. There is currently a big case being vetted and the mistake the collector made was to completely trust a few unscrupulous dealers without doing his own research nor studying, nor surrounding himself with experts, nor being a part of various collecting organizations wherein one learns by association with those who know fakes when they see them. The modern collector must do his homework; I read almost every night books on the subjects I collect, have now been doing it for 61 years and still I learn every day and from every collector friend. The best thing a collector can do is show his collection to others and ask for their opinions.

EW: In addition to several books that you have authored in the field of Western antiques, you have recently co-authored with historian Roy B. Young the new book Chasing Billy the Kid: Frank Stewart and the Untold Story of the Manhunt for William H. Bonney. What attracted you to the story of the Kid?

KH: The reason I became attracted to the story of Billy the Kid is as amazing as it was unpredictable. I purchased an old pistol (shown on the cover of the book) which has a mysterious monogram for an individual and then I learned that it was one of a pair and the other pistol which belongs to a friend of mine which had more information on the presentation of the pair to an individual which was unfamiliar to me, being a novice at the time on Billy the Kid history. Ironically, I was not a Billy the Kid fan; I thought there was little or nothing remaining unknown about Billy the Kid, so I omitted him from my areas of interest leaving him to the experts. Then I discovered the identity of the individual and the plot thickened; for me it is a desire to know the history of an item that pushes me into an investigation of its milieu, or its owner. Sometimes artifacts corroborate the history and other times history verifies the artifacts.

EW: Let's talk about Frank Stewart. Who was he and how does he play into the story of Billy the Kid?

KH: We soon discovered that Frank Stewart was the mysterious recipient of the fancy pistols, and the story was published in contemporary New Mexico newspapers during the 1880's so when I realized that Frank Stewart was equally responsible with Pat Garrett in the capture of Billy the Kid, I wondered why Frank Stewart never received any credit for the deed, because all accounts assign the credit to Pat Garrett. As our book reveals, Frank Stewart deserves equal credit for the successful chase and capture of the Kid, but he has never been adequately recognized. More surprisingly Frank Stewart was not his real name! In a 1932 Amarillo newspaper he revealed himself as John Green, a stock detective hired by Charles Goodnight and the Canadian River Cattlemen's Association to recover their stolen cattle and capture the thieves, which turned out to be Billy the Kid. As a detective, he did not want to use his real name, so hardly anyone knew who he really was until the 1932 newspaper reveal.

EW: Why is Pat Garrett remembered today, but Frank Stewart all but forgotten?

KH: Simply put, the main reason Pat Garrett is remembered today is because he was the man who killed The Kid. If Frank Stewart had killed him, you might not even know who Pat Garrett was. Too, Pat Garrett's book, *The Authentic Life of Billy the Kid....* with the help of Ash Upson was about the first account published only a little over a year after the killing, in 1882, and it became the most popular source of information for hungry readers.

EW: Describe your research and writing process. Also, how was it working with Roy B. Young?

KH: Research and writing... well, I know my own limitations so I immediately enlisted the help of my good friend Roy Young who had just retired and asked him to help me track down the mysterious "Frank Stewart" as I knew him, and as anyone who knows Roy can attest, he is the *best* researcher, and without his tenacity and writing ability, I might never have accomplished the book. I could not have done it without Roy; he was absolutely the *best* partner, the best researcher and writer, I cannot say enough good about Roy except that he is *the best*! We each had our areas of expertise and I needed Roy, fortunately we made a good team. After five years of working together you get to know your partner; (e.g., Roy likes pie).

EW: Had you always intended to pursue a project on Billy the Kid?

KH: No, as I mentioned earlier, oddly, I had little interest in Billy the Kid until I obtained the gun, then the gun made the story come alive for me and I wanted to know more, and when Roy and I realized the lack of credit given Frank Stewart, we resolved to do a book which would give him recognition and right this wrong in publication.

EW: What challenges did you and your co-author encounter while researching the book?

KH: As for challenges we encountered, the first big one was discovering the real identity of Frank Stewart; that surprise sent the story into a different direction like the plot of a good movie. I think it was at that point Roy said, "Kurt, we are gonna have to do a book on this" because we both realized it was a big error of recorded history. Another challenge was producing many results from investigating The Canadian River Cattlemen's Association which quickly evolved into the Panhandle Plains Cattlemen's Association. Most of the literature either omitted or denied the role of that organization yet we found it especially important. Another challenge was locating the other gun of the pair! Talk about serendipity, the way we found it after a year-long search is an amazing story itself involving other friends and even Roy's wife Charlotte!

EW: Any plans for future projects with Roy Young? If so, can you talk more about them?

KH: Future projects with Roy? Are you kidding? I welcome the chance to again collaborate with my esteemed friend, as I have said, he is simply **the best** partner, co-author a writer can have, even wish for. I feel blessed that he consented, that he became as interested in the story as I was, and we could not have had a better joint effort; incredibly, we agreed on almost every decision of the book's production. We laugh about it today, how much we think alike, and if any author has the chance to work with Roy, do it! But those members of the Wild West History Association already know what great skill sets Roy has, easy on the trigger, calm and deliberate, and all the while so affable during stressful or tense times. I would do another project with Roy in a heartbeat; we are considering projects on some Lincoln County War participants about which little is known, such as Billie Wilson, who was one of Billy's best friends, but who was actually David L. Anderson that ended up a lawman in Texas.

Matthew S. Luckett is a professor at Sierra College in California and is the recent author of the recent book *Never Caught Twice: Horse Stealing in Western Nebraska, 1850-1890*. Luckett holds a Ph.D. in history from the University of California and is currently working on a new project focusing on the New Madrid Earthquakes.

EW (Erik Wright): Your new book *Never Caught Twice: Horse Stealing in Western Nebraska, 1850-1890* presents a surgical look at livestock raids, rustling, and thievery on the high plains. What led you to investigate this story?

MSL (Matthew S. Luckett): When I started my graduate training at UCLA, I was originally interested in studying anti-horse thief societies and other vigilante responses to horse stealing. However, for me a big part of that story was understanding why horse stealing was so maligned in the first place. Although Americans today already seem to believe that horse theft was a severe problem in late-Nineteenth Century rural America, I wanted numbers. As my research focused increasingly on finding horse thieves rather than anti-horse thief societies, my dissertation adviser very sensibly suggested that if I was going to spend so much time researching horse thieves, I might as well write about them instead. Needless to say, I took his advice, and soon I realized just how little we actually know about horse stealing as a crime and as a broader phenomenon.

EW: What does horse theft in western Nebraska tell us about outlawry and rustling in the other parts of the west?

MSL: Western Nebraska was representative of the Great Plains region in general, and in many ways, it was the crossroads of America at that point in time: the Overland Trail and Union Pacific Railroad together formed the most important and most heavily used trans-continental route in the United States, while the Texas, Bozeman, and Sidney-Black Hills Trails connected this road to cattle ranches in the south and gold fields to the north and west. It was a hunting and camping ground for the Oglala and Brule Lakota, the Northern Cheyenne, the Pawnees, the Otoes, and other Plains Indian nations, as well as an operational theater for the United States Army for over two decades. Fur traders, road ranchers, cattlemen, homesteaders, and Exodusters all made homes here, while hundreds of thousands of migrants and their livestock passed through the area while on their way to Oregon, California, and Utah. Yet despite the region's diversity, all of these groups owned, possessed, or utilized horses in one way or another. Horses were universally valuable, whether or not one was a Plains Indian or a white cattle rancher, a farmer or a business executive. In that sense, western Nebraska was an ideal microcosm for understanding how horse stealing affected all of these different groups, and how each of those different groups responded to – or rolled with – horse stealing culture.

EW: What types of horse thieves were there? What were their motivations?

MSL: The most important thing to understand is that when people today think of a "horse thief," they usually imagine someone swinging at the end of a rope. They might conjure up a common criminal, someone evil enough to take another person's most valuable possession yet dumb enough to get caught. Or, weirdly enough, they might imagine one of their ancestors, since I cannot count the number of times one person or another has told me, "My great grandpa was a horse thief, or at least we all think he was." I don't know what that says about their family, but I've heard this from a lot of folks.

In truth, people stole horses for a whole host of reasons. Plains Indians engaged in a reciprocal horse raiding culture, in which horse stealing was a conduit to gaining revenge, counting coup, and acquiring wealth and prestige. But according to Wooden Leg, a Northern Cheyenne warrior who fought at the Battle of the Greasy Grass (Little Bighorn), horse jealousies sometimes led to fighting among the Cheyenne over the most prized horses, and a few of these instances led to murder. Among the whites, many horses were stolen by quintessential bad guys and bandits – the Doc Middleton gang alone stole as many as four thousand horses from ranches and Plains Indians alike – but they were also stolen by less-likely criminals, such as soldiers attempting to desert their isolated posts, ranchers filing fraudulent claims for Indian ponies seized by the Army, and farmers facing destitution amid bad harvests and mounting debts. Cowboys, who were not well-paid and were often disrespected by their employers, stole horses as well. Meanwhile, some horse stealing accusations were trumped-up charges stemming from other criminal or civil matters. In one case, a man accused a livery owner of stealing his horse, when in reality the livery owner was simply repossessing the animal after the man defaulted on his horse mortgage.

EW: What was the law-and-order response to horse theft during this period? Could it be compared to auto theft by today's standards?

MSL: Law enforcers did what they could, but they could not do much. In western Nebraska, sheriffs, police, and other agencies had extremely limited resources and huge, sprawling areas to patrol. Also, the purpose of law enforcement at that time was not to prevent crime, but to apprehend those responsible for committing it. Citizens were generally on their own when determining how to protect their animals. As a result, there is a great deal of supplemental, extralegal law enforcement and organized vigilantism in western Nebraska. Their responses range from stockmen associations hiring brand detectives and patrolling outbound freight trains for stolen stock to mobs, vigilante societies, and even newspapers issuing threats to local criminals to leave the area or face the business end of a noose.

As for the auto theft comparison, horses were vastly more indispensable since they were a means of transportation, a means of production, a hard-to-replace investment in a cash-poor economy, and a much-loved pet. If someone stole my car I would be upset, but I would also be able to walk or Uber home. I could then rent a car until I recover or replace my old one. In 1880s Nebraska, if someone stole your horses, or your horses died, and you were a farmer, then you would be in deep trouble. Most folks did not have $40 on hand to go buy another horse, which is why so many people mortgaged or borrowed their teams.

I recently saw someone on social media compare a stolen horse 120 years ago to a stolen dog today. I would actually combine the two analogies: imagine loving your car in the same way you love your dog and needing your dog in the same way you need your car. That's basically what it meant to own – and lose – a horse.

EW: Your book covers a wide spectrum of players from outlaws to the American to the United States military. What challenges did you face in your research and how did you remain disciplined in your focus?

MSL: Well, for one, the research logistics were often difficult. My primary source research was pretty far-flung, so I did a lot of traveling for this book. I made several trips to the National Archives in Washington, DC to collect and photograph thousands of pages of Army documents, and I spent several months between the Autry Library in Burbank, California and the Nebraska State Historical Society in Lincoln doing research. But while these trips were usually a lot of fun, the best part of my research was having to travel throughout western Nebraska. Most of my legal records live in local county courthouses, so I would usually have to contact the county or district court clerks in advance to work out a time for me to come by and go through their historical records. And these court clerks are some of the nicest, hardest-working people I've ever met, and they were always gracious enough to let this guy from California spread out on a table and rifle through 150-year-old ledger books. In addition to that I toured local libraries and museums, took a lot of photographs for the book, and visited several of the sites I discuss in the book, like Fort Robinson and the Boot Hill Cemetery in Sidney. This was by far the coolest and most rewarding part of my research adventure.

On a more macro level, I had to become an expert on many different subjects, while also knowing that I would never *be* "an expert" on any one of them. However, when writing an academic history book, there is little margin for error. Not being an expert on a particular subject is not an excuse for being wrong. So, I consulted a lot of people throughout this process, and this book would not have been possible without the help of numerous colleagues who have corrected me on innumerable occasions. But historical writing and research is always a balancing act. Global subjects often lack a certain amount of detail and nuance, while narrow and local subjects tend to be more myopic and less relevant outside their immediate area. For my own book, I tried to keep my focus on horse stealing and avoid tumbling down too many rabbit holes that strayed away from that larger narrative. While there are a lot of moving parts, many of which are no doubt already familiar to your readers, I think they all come together to tell a fresh story that has not yet been told.

EW: Did widespread horse theft change the culture of high plains society in any fundamental way? If so, how?

MSL: Yes, it did, both in the short-term and in the long-term.

The short-term consequences were more hazardous than most historians realize. Horse stealing was both a culture and a crisis on the Great Plains. It was a culture in that various groups across the region, including Plains Indians, ranchers, and even the Army, legitimized horse theft (or "seizure," as was often the case with the latter) as a necessary activity. But it was also a crisis: conflicts over stolen livestock sparked two wars along the

Overland Trail, while horse raids sometimes led to much more violent confrontations. Elsewhere, horse stealing fears led to friction within, as well as bad blood between, various groups. Victims of horse stealing suffered in myriad ways, from homesteaders having to vacate their claims to Plains Indian nations not having enough horses on hand to hunt or defend themselves. It is difficult to understate just how devastating horse stealing was to communities across the Great Plains, and how impossible it was to end it.

In the long-term, I think horse stealing contributed both psychologically and culturally to our society's tendency to treat property crime as a social and moral evil that justifies an extralegal response. For instance, horse stealing was not the only problem horse owners faced. When I reviewed prominent Nebraska rancher John Bratt's horse records, I discovered that he lost far more horses from premature death than through theft. Dozens of his horses died from snakebites, lighting strikes, exposure, passing trains, or disease, while he only reported six being stolen. Some farmers overworked their animals to the point of death, while other horses badly broke their legs and were put down. More broadly, farmers and ranchers faced bone-chilling winter storms, floods, droughts, prairie fires, falling commodity prices, rising freight fares, and even locust swarms. All these problems affected their livelihood, but out of all of them, only horse thieves could be caught, blamed, punished, and scapegoated. After all, one cannot hang a locust or imprison a lightning strike. And today, many Americans continue to scapegoat criminals and other individuals as the source of their problems, even though I would wager that the biggest problems they and Americans by and large face are more institutional and structural in nature. While horse thieves are not the first criminal bogeyman in American history, they are one of the most enduring. And one of the reasons why we know so little about them is because it is difficult for us to disentangle the reality of what a horse thief was from the shadowy, anonymous, evil character we typically imagine.

EW: What role did vigilante groups play in helping to keep the peace in the great plains? Were these groups a direct reaction to horse theft?

MSL: First of all, to address a common myth: contrary to popular belief, most horse thieves were never hanged, nor were there any states to my knowledge that legally made horse stealing a capital crime. That was certainly the case in both Nebraska and Texas, although I have not researched the laws against horse stealing in other states. Moreover, although virtually all horse thieves who were hanged were lynched by private citizens, not very many horse thieves were hanged in the first place. Between 1867 and 1950, for instance, Nebraskans hanged nine men for stealing horses. By way of comparison, Nebraskans accused or charged thousands of men with the crime during that time.

Beyond that, as I noted above, vigilante groups played a significant role, along with Federal marshals, sheriffs, police, night watchmen, private detectives, stock inspectors, and even (before 1877) the Army, in responding to horse theft. Some groups, like the anti-horse thief associations that attracted hundreds of thousands of members after the Civil War, were formed directly in response to horse stealing. But there is little evidence to suggest, at least in western Nebraska, that most vigilante groups helped "keep the peace" in any meaningful way. Apart from threats of and calls for lethal violence, which were often published in local newspapers, most extralegal organizations sought to either prevent theft before it happened or assist local law enforcement in apprehending suspects afterward. In those places where people were hanged for horse stealing, as when both Kid Wade and his father were killed in the Niobrara Valley, local residents were deeply suspicious of local law enforcement and suspected that county officials were also guilty of rustling. For most other would-be vigilantes, however, these groups provided little more than a watchful presence on dark nights and a feeling of control over something as calamitous and fateful as a stolen horse.

    Just as many Americans today imagine horse thieves to be unrepentant criminals and not as a wide and diverse lot of people who stole horses within a legal and moral culture that by and large allowed them to do so, we also tend to imagine most vigilantes as either being paragons of virtue who wanted to keep their communities safe, or as evil people in their own right. No doubt some vigilantes were evil and lynching across the Jim Crow South in particular was disgusting, unconscionable, and utterly lacking in any moral justification. But I think that most of the folks who joined anti-horse thief societies, or who whispered among themselves that horse thieves should by all rights be hanged, were not inherently evil or even violent people. Nor did these groups pop up in response to a lack of functional law enforcement. They were simply trying to cope with an intractable problem that threatened to bankrupt them and render their families stranded or homeless. Members would meet at a pub, a school, or even a church, puff out their chests and commit to sending out organized patrols of the area, and go home believing that they had done something constructive to protect themselves, their property, and their communities. And it may well have been their neighbor, a friendly though down-on-his-luck farmer sitting quietly among them during the meeting, who stole the horses in the first place.

Matthew Bernstein is the author of *George Hearst: Silver King of the Gilded Age* and the more recent *Hanging Charley Flinn: The Short and Violent Life of the Boldest Criminal in Frontier California*. He works as a professor of English at Los Angeles City College and is the editor of the Wild West History Association *Journal*.

EW (Erik Wright): Who was George Hearst?

MB (Matthew Bernstein): George Hearst was the greatest miner of the Old West. After leaving Missouri in 1850, he scored mild successes in the California gold rush, then became a millionaire through silver in the early days of Virginia City in Nevada Territory. Losing his fortune through bad stock investments, he rebounded with a silver mine outside Salt Lake City, then expanded his fortune through gold in Deadwood and copper in Montana. In respect to mining, described in basketball terms, Hearst was like a combination of Michael Jordan and Lebron

James. He had Michael's competitive spirit mixed with Lebron's ability to succeed in different environments.

Hearst's final act played out in Washington D.C. Appointed to the United States Senate in 1886, Hearst was kicked out of office by Republicans who deemed his appointment unconstitutional. Winning the senatorial election that followed, he returned to the Capitol Building. Hearst and his philanthropic wife Phoebe bought a mansion a mile from the Executive Mansion, where they lived the glamorous life of Gilded Age millionaires.

EW: Describe his early years and how those initial experiences may have influenced Hearst's decisions later in life.

MB: Growing up on a Missouri farm sixty miles southwest of St. Louis, Hearst's education was patchy. He spent a few months at a time in log cabins, learning reading, writing, and arithmetic. Mostly he learned from his mother and father how to manage the family farm. When he and his father sold good to French miners, Hearst saw how much money could be made. Shortly afterwards, he began working the lead mine on the farm and attended night classes at a local mining school.

In his memoir, Hearst also revealed he was his "mother's boy," and took more after her, a practical, managing woman. However, in several ways Hearst took after his father, emulating and then outshining his father in the political arena.

EW: What impact did Hearst have on the development of mining in the frontier west?

MB: The old saying "It takes a mine to work a mine" was very true in the frontier. Once Hearst had established himself as a millionaire, he could swing enough capital to build up not just a mine, but a mining town, and a mining region. This meant community commerce: railroads, restaurants, storefronts, and schoolhouses. At the same time, Hearst's motives were capitalistic rather than charitable. As a red-blooded American, Hearst was expected by his San Francisco partners to secure mining rights, water rights, and railroad rights at all costs. In short, not everyone benefited from Hearst's presence.

EW: Despite his importance no full-length biography has been written prior to your book. Why do you think he has been ignored by previous historians?

MB: Although George Hearst was a larger-than-life character—the most recognizable miner in the Old West, a United States Senator, and a friend to Mark Twain—the notoriety of his flamboyant son, William Randolph Hearst, largely eclipsed him in the twentieth century. Of the dozens of biographies on W. R. Hearst, most treated George as a prologue character in his son's life story. The HBO series *Deadwood* and Gerald McRaney's portrayal of him deserve credit for bringing Hearst back into the American consciousness.

EW: Talk about his relationship with son media magnate William Randolph Hearst.

MB: Like George taking after his mother, William Randolph Hearst gravitated towards his own mother, Phoebe. This was largely because through long stretches of W. R.'s childhood, George was in the Wild West, trying to raise another fortune. W. R., like George before him, wanted to emulate and outshine his father. It quickly became apparent to W. R. that working as a mining operator bored him, but his father did own a flagging newspaper, *The San Francisco Examiner*. This sparked an interest in W. R. that turned into a forest fire. Although at first George was concerned that his boy's newspaper would never pay, when after three years it began turning a profit, George admitted to being proud of W. R. Certainly, W. R. Hearst was proud as well.

Another aspect that W. R. inherited from his father was his culinary taste. W. R. made certain rich foods were always available at La Cuesta Encantada, better known as Hearst Castle, and riding horses and playing cowboy was one of his favorite delights. W. R. also inherited his father's financial sense: spend money like water, because you can always make another fortune.

EW: Let's talk about your research and writing process. We've established the importance of Hearst in the context of western history, but what challenges did you encounter in writing about him?

MB: Separating the real Hearst from the false praise was my first research challenge. Because Hearst died a senator, members of Congress delivered various speeches, making Hearst out to be the greatest American since Paul Bunyan: heroic, noble, charitable, and just the cat's pajamas. Naturally, his first biographers, Cora and Fremont Older, who were friends of the Hearst family, also took this tack, painting Hearst as a flawless, fun-loving titan. To find the real Hearst, I combed through the Hearst business papers, letters, contemporary accounts, and visited his old stomping grounds. In actuality, Hearst could be quite the rascal.

Another challenge was recognizing the "tall tale" effect that Hearst generated. One particularly noteworthy example was a *New York Times*, Christmas Day article that waxed nostalgic on the friendship of Mark Twain and George Hearst in Virginia City. It's a wild story, ending where Hearst gets into a bareknuckle boxing match at a wedding, and when Hearst is knocked unconscious the guests hilariously find out that George is wearing Mark's shirt. Such stories are fun but aren't real.

EW: How would a man like Hearst fit in today's society and business climate?

MB: One of Senator Hearst's passions was protecting California's forests, and during his lifetime it was said that only John Muir was more instrumental in establishing Yosemite National Park. Today, Hearst would be a full-fledged advocate for combatting the fires that have been devastating California's forests. Additionally, considering Hearst loved wild and natural environs, protecting, preserving, and visiting America's wilderness would be natural for him.

EW: Hearst was present at some of the most wild and violent boomtowns on the frontier including Deadwood and Pioche, Nevada. Did he encounter troubles in these towns?

MB: In both Deadwood and Pioche Hearst was seen as an invader. In Deadwood he secured rights to the greatest gold mine in the Black Hills, the Homestake mine, but when a boundary dispute erupted between his guards and the Pride of the West guards, one of the Homestake guards shot and killed a Pride of the West man. Hearst raced back to Deadwood to deal with the murder trial. When the jury voted to acquit the Hearst guard, the judge and newspapermen make public their belief that Hearst had bribed the jury.

Hearst was involved in another scandalous trial in Pioche, also involving a boundary dispute. When his miners dug into a rival mineshaft, a jury was called to determine who could claim the silver. It was said that Hearst bribed the jury "like sausages." Hearst recalled making $250,000 as a result—about 5 million in today's money.

EW: What is the connection between Hearst and the Sherlock Holmes story "The Problem of Thor Bridge" first published in 1922?

MB: In this murder mystery, Holmes is hired by Neil Gibson, a senator from "some western state" and "The Gold King." Many people have speculated that, based on that, Gibson is based on George Hearst. Gibson's dead Brazilian wife, however, bears no resemblance to Phoebe Hearst. Incidentally, the short story first appeared in his son's publication, *Hearst's International Magazine*.

More plausible is that Jack London, who wrote up the debut of the Hearst Memorial Mining Building at UC Berkeley for *The San Francisco Examiner*, based the miner in his short story "All Gold Canyon" off of Hearst. The miner is described as "sandy-complexioned" with hair "sparse and unkempt" and eyes that were "startling blue

... laughing and merry," and that those eyes contained "calm self-reliance and strength of purpose." Joel and Ethan Coen's 2018 film *The Ballad of Buster Scruggs* beautifully brings London's short story to life. And in a way, brings Hearst to life as well.

Matthew Hulbert is a historian and Elliott Associate Professor of History at Hampden-Sydney College in Virginia. He is the author of *Oracle of Lost Causes: John Newman Edwards and His Never-Ending Civil War* and *The Ghosts of Guerrilla Memory: How Civil War Bushwhackers Became Gunslingers in the American West*.

EW (Erik Wright): Is this work a continuation of your earlier writing *The Ghosts of Guerrilla Memory: How Civil War Guerrillas Became Gunslingers in the American West* (Univ. of Georgia Press, 2016)?

MH (Matthew Hulbert): Yes, that's definitely a fair assessment. *Ghosts* is a chronicle of how and why we've remembered—and, in some cases, how we've been programmed *not* to remember—Civil War guerrillas. It would be impossible to tell that story without John Newman Edwards. He was the architect of an irregular Lost Cause in Missouri designed around bushwhackers and he laid the foundation for how future generations of historians would approach guerrilla war in the western borderlands. In many ways, for better or worse, we're still responding to him today. Even so, the real stars of *Ghosts* are the memory narratives themselves; they are ultimately what reveal distinctly American ideas about identity and violence.

In *Oracle of Lost Causes*, John Newman Edwards finally gets his turn on the marquee. His work on irregular warfare, exemplified by *Noted Guerrillas* (1877), is important, but it's now one piece of a much broader puzzle. Edwards isn't a household name in the twenty-first century, so what makes that puzzle worthwhile—and his personal story so astounding—is its Forrest Gump-like quality. He is the common thread running through the accounts of so many A-list historical characters. Collectively, his saga weaves those threads into a grand tapestry of nineteenth-century politics and culture. And what does the tapestry show us? The Civil War gets much bigger geographically—it becomes part of a continental and then an international struggle. In turn, the war's outcome takes on additional meaning in the American West and within conservative political circles around the world.

EW: Why has Arthur McCoy become totally forgotten about today? He was part of the "Terrible Quintette" and deserves more attention from historians, or does he not?

MH: Of the outlaws profiled in "A Terrible Quintette" (1873), Arthur McCoy's infamy had by far the shortest shelf-life. Even most historians of the West probably wouldn't recall his story without a little help. There are a few factors that help explain why he more or less disappears. Not surprisingly, John Newman Edwards had quite a bit to do with it.

To start, McCoy wasn't a Civil War bushwhacker. That being the case, he lacked a significant shared experience with other core members of the gang—and even with primary associates like Allen Parmer, Clell Miller, and Jim Cummins. (John Younger, it's worth nothing, was too young to join Quantrill's bushwhackers during the war, but his entire family was effectively engulfed by the guerrilla war.) As the James-Younger Gang became increasingly notorious and increasingly wanted by law enforcement, members relied extensively on bonds formed fighting in the brush. McCoy became less important and, frankly, was probably *never* as important as "A Terrible Quintette" made him out to be in 1873. He faded from the foreground of the gang and wasn't even present for the disastrous, 1876 raid at Northfield, Minnesota.

Edwards played a major role in turning the James-Younger Gang into a national sensation when it suited his political purposes. But as public sentiment changed and social banditry fell out of vogue, he shifted his focus to guerrillas and Civil War memory. This meant that Jesse and Frank James, along with Cole Younger and other former bandits, received a second commemorative life while McCoy, who had nothing to do with the guerrilla war, continued his slide into obscurity.

Now whether Arthur McCoy deserves more attention from historians is another matter. To quote William Munny in *Unforgiven* (1992), "deserves got nuthin' to do with it." By that I mean historians have likely overlooked McCoy due to a lack of source material, not because he wasn't interesting enough to warrant coverage.

EW: If John Newman Edwards contributed so much for Civil War buffs and/or "gunslingers" history, why has he not been the subject of full biographies before now? What has he lacked?

MH: This is a question I get asked all the time, especially once people learn a little about John Newman Edwards. In addition to the political and historical significances you've already mentioned, the man lived one hell of a life. The short version: he fought in the Civil War, served time as a POW, lived in Mexican exile for two years, embroiled himself in political and editorial feuds, fought a duel, helped Frank James surrender, and found himself in rehab for alcoholism multiple times. So, I think the answer actually has less to do with what he lacked than with finding a way to effectively deal with *so much* in a single, cohesive narrative.

From a source perspective, Edwards also presents a unique situation. He left behind a voluminous archive of writing. We're talking books, editorials, reviews, letters, adjutant reports, legal documents, and much more. But virtually all of these texts are focused on other people, which is to say, Edwards produced thousands of pages and only a tiny fraction of them are autobiographical. This is why he's featured prominently in biographies of Joseph Orville Shelby and Jesse James—figures he helped make famous with his pen—as the man behind the proverbial curtain. However, to use Edwards's writing as the foundation for his own biography necessitated reading extensively between the lines, dissecting myths (that he created!), and immense amounts of background research on all of the stories that intersect it. My hunch is that these requirements have acted as a deterrent over the years, and I'd be lying if I said I wasn't fortunate they had.

EW: Did John Newman Edwards' alcoholism contribute to his devoting himself to lost causes? If his alcoholism had not been so severe, would he still have been an "oracle" of lost causes?

MH: As a preface, it's worth mentioning that Edwards was hardly alone in his addiction to "the monster of drink." Myriad Civil War veterans—including men who'd experienced far less battlefield trauma than Edwards—took to self-medicating in the aftermath of the conflict. This was an era in which medical professionals lacked any awareness of psychological ailments like Shell Shock or PTSD. And equally problematic, gender standards in the late nineteenth century deemed outward expressions of emotional trauma as signs of weakness and defect in men.

Toward the end of his life, following multiple failed attempts to quit drinking, Edwards understood *himself* to be something of a lost cause. His letters from this period dripped sadness and self-loathing. Yet my sense is not that his personal failings with liquor contributed significantly to the brand of nostalgic, reactionary politics that defined his life. The loss of his father at such a formative moment and the mythologies he employed to fill the void set him on a backward-looking track long before he could uncork a bottle. Then his life essentially unfolds as an impossible quest not only to halt modernity, but to recreate an idealized version of the Old World that had never existed in the first place. Thus, his drinking became a mechanism for coping with political and cultural causes that remained lost despite his best efforts to restore them.

EW: One might be tempted to describe the divisiveness in today's American society with John Newman Edwards' stand in his day. You write: "Now he was unequivocally justifying the action of the James-Younger Gang as an insurgency against unjust government policies; now John glorified the former guerrillas as men willing to take a violent stand on behalf of all downtrodden southerners." (p. 186) Is the United States today becoming a parallel to the way Edwards viewed the direction U.S. was taking?

MH: I can understand why it might be tempting to view Edwards as a bellwether for divisiveness in contemporary politics or to gauge whether society is devolving back into a more violent version of itself. But here I would offer a historian's caution: when we approach the past with a specific answer already in mind, we're almost always going to find what we want to hear—not necessarily what we need to hear.

In this case, what we probably need to hear from the saga of John Newman Edwards is a simple but stark reminder: from slave insurrections and Indian genocides to the Civil War to race riots to draft riots to dynamite-toting coalminers to spectacle lynchings to vigilante executions to Oklahoma City and Waco, we've *always* been divided politically, and our society has *always* been violent. What's allowed us to forget about these ugly episodes are the stories we tell about ourselves—the way we collectively remember the American Experience. One of the most important payloads of Edwards's story is a behind-the-scenes look at how those memory narratives are designed and how they compete for dominance in the public consciousness.

EW: Can you discuss a bit more about your earlier book *The Ghosts of Guerrilla Memory* and what inspired you to write it?

MH: I grew up fascinated with cowboys and gunslingers and, not surprisingly, I absolutely loved westerns. With that in mind, two realizations prompted me to write *Ghosts*. First, that some of these cowboys and gunmen had deep roots in the American Civil War. And second, that several of them had not actually been cowboys or gunslingers at all. So, like historians, I set out to answer a question: why did Americans remember the Jameses and the Youngers as icons of the Wild West rather than as diehard Confederate bushwhackers who hailed from slave-owning families in Missouri?

What I eventually discovered is that in the 1870s and 1880s, as elite ex-Confederates in Richmond and New Orleans set out to define how the war would be remembered on terms most generous to the defeated South, they had no use for wild-haired, pistol-packing, scalp-taking bushwhackers. These irregulars simply didn't fit the narrative of chivalrous gentlemen waging a civilized war on behalf of lofty political principles. So, through histories and dime novels, borderland guerrillas were effectively excommunicated to the Wild West—a place where their brand of "savage" violence served a more useful purpose in the story of the American frontier and Manifest Destiny. After the turn of the twentieth century, as cultural mediums evolved, dime novels and pulp histories gave way to movies and television. Once the James-Younger crew became mainstays of the western genre, their place in the mythology of a West they'd never actually experienced became permanent.

EW: Could the men of James-Younger Gang be viewed as the prototype for the Western gunman?

MH: This is a fascinating question because it forces us to reckon simultaneously with Civil War memory and cherished myths of the Western frontier. On one hand, popular culture tells us that "yes," Jesse James, especially, fits the mold of a Western shootist perfectly. On the other hand, however, well-sourced history gives us an emphatic "no!"

In spite of what dime novels, pop histories, TV shows, and western films would have us believe, Jesse James never really operated in the same "Wild West" space as bona fide gunhands like Billy the Kid, Tom Horn, Wyatt Earp, Doc Holiday, Bill Hickok, Dallas Stoudenmire, or John Wesley Hardin. He was never involved in range wars, mining disputes, rough-and-tumble cow towns, or Indian fighting. And neither was his brother Frank, nor were any of the Younger brothers, who together formed the effective core of the James-Younger Gang during its heyday in the mid-1870s.

That said, if we want to look at the scenario hypothetically—and pretend for a moment that Jesse James or Cole Younger rubbed shoulders with Horn or Holliday or Hardin—the James-Younger boys would almost certainly have held their own. They spent years waging, and surviving, a brutal irregular conflict. They emerged from the Civil War as elite horsemen and near-peerless revolver shots. Better still, they were unafraid to claim human lives when they believed their own survival depended on it.

EW: What projects do you have planned next for book-length treatments?

MH: At the moment, I'm writing a new, narrative history of the Lawrence Massacre. Many of your readers probably know the basics of the story: on August 21, 1863, William Quantrill and a few hundred Missouri bushwhackers thundered into Lawrence, Kansas, gunned down nearly 200 men and boys, and torched much of the city. The attack has been remembered as the most infamous guerrilla raid of the entire Civil War and as one of the most outlandish moments in American military history.

My coverage of the massacre involves several new sources but also prioritizes the perspectives of westerners who largely experienced the Civil War as an irregular conflict. Reassessed from that vantage, the raid takes on a new meaning. I don't want to give away too much before even finishing the book, but most of the elements of the Lawrence Massacre that historians have argued made it anomalous within the guerrilla war *were not* why it struck westerners and veterans of irregular violence as unique. Ultimately, this is another, albeit deeper exploration of "American violence."

After Lawrence, the plan is to tell the story of the lever-action rifle's place in American history and culture—from the Civil War, the Indian Wars, and the Wild West to hunting camps across the country and then onto the Silver Screen. Given recent political debates about access to firearms, civilian vs. military weapons technology, and the place of big game hunting in contemporary American society, the rise and fall of these rifles has the potential to tell us far more about ourselves than just how we "won the West."

Mark Boardman is editor of *The Tombstone Epitaph* and features editor for *True West* magazine. Boardman is a leader in the field of Western history publications and has helped numerous authors and historians over the decades in their research. He is also the pastor of Poplar Grove United Methodist Church in Avon, Indiana.

EW (Erik Wright): Mark, you wear many hats: editor at *The Tombstone Epitaph*, features editor at *True West* magazine, pastor, husband, and grandfather. How do you juggle all these responsibilities?

MB (Mark Boardman): Sometimes, not very well. Especially during those weeks where I have deadlines for both publications, in addition to completing assignments for continuing education, in addition to preparing two worship services. It helps that I'm a fast writer—and that, on occasion, there can be a crossover. I've researched and written some Old West stories that I also used as the basis for sermons. But that doesn't happen often.

EW: Let's talk about you when you were young or at least the age when you first became interested in Western history?

MB: I grew up in the sixties when prime time television was dominated by Westerns. I'd sit in front of the TV with my dad and just take it all in. I'd play cowboys and Indians, emulating the stories and characters I saw every night. I had no idea that most of the shows were pure fiction; I just knew I enjoyed them. About 25 years ago, I discovered the National Outlaw and Lawman History Association (NOLA) and the Western Outlaw and Lawman History Association (WOLA; these two organizations have merged and are now the Wild West History Association). I got involved and began learning about the true history of that time and space. And it fascinated me even more than stuff like *The Life and Legend of Wyatt Earp*. I became hooked. But as I grew up, I became interested in other things. Reading about Old West history was a hobby, something very secondary in my life. Little did I know that I would come back to it.

EW: How did that interest transform itself into a career?

MB: In 1997, I'd basically blown up my previous career in public radio. I was looking for something to do (and hoped there'd be some pay involved). NOLA had published a series of books, and the organization's President Lee Simmons asked if I'd be interested in promoting and selling them. I was and did. I was also introduced to Bob Boze Bell of *True West*. He'd just been involved in the purchase of the magazine and was looking for bright and talented people to help out. Instead, he got me. Seriously, I kept pushing him until they hired me as features editor; I started on my 50th birthday, and that was one of the best birthdays I ever had. And as I approach 17 years with *True West*, it's hard to believe that it's the longest job I've ever held. I certainly couldn't have imagined that when I was five years old and watching Bat Masterson on TV.

EW: Is there an intersection between your passion for Wild West history and your role as a pastor?

MB: Yes. One of my first-ever sermons was on the Old West—and I dressed the part, with boots and cowboy hat (no guns, of course). And the response was much better than I'd ever imagined. But there are some great conversion stories. Union bomber Harry Orchard turned to Seventh Day Adventism after he'd been caught. Cole Younger liked to attend tent revivals and speak, giving a "crime does not pay" message. I've also been fascinated by the story of the family of Andrew Trew Blachly. He was killed in a botched Colorado bank robbery attempt. Somehow, his widow (who had a very strong faith) managed to raise eight sons on her own. And she made sure every one of them went to college. Their success in life was directly attributable to Dellie Blachly's drive, wisdom, and faith. I'm still amazed by that story—and it works in the Old West publications as well as in a worship message.

EW: You have been in the field of Western history now for many years (no offense). What changes have you seen occur during that time?

MB: I've seen our greatest generation pass on; these were people who did Old West research and writing on the side, beyond their professions, often without formal training in historiography, and had the gall to question some of the traditional sources. In doing so, they corrected so much of what is known about Western characters. Many others have taken up the task and are doing a great job. But nobody can replace the men and women who uncovered the truth.

EW: Where do you see the future of the field going in the next 10, 20, or 50 years?

MB: I'm not sure. Things are changing so quickly--and I fear it may not be good. Major publishers are cutting back on books, which means that some worthy efforts may not come out. The era of video games, social media, and other things that young people do on their phones does not bode well for the field. We have yet to find a way to transfer things to the new realities. And the continuing rise of conspiracy theories means the field must do an even better job of presenting the facts in an open, compelling, and understandable fashion—or else people will believe the myths.

EW: Let's discuss *The Tombstone Epitaph*. How did you get involved with the most famous publication in Arizona's history?

MB: About five years ago, my predecessor decided to retire. Our owner, Bob Love, reached out to *True West*'s Bob Boze Bell for any editor recommendations. Boze tossed my name out—and then he contacted me to admit to what he'd done. Bob Love and I connected, began discussions, and eventually I was hired. Sometimes it's who you know.... I think that I still owe Boze dinner (and much more) for that favor.

EW: What is a day in the life at *The Epitaph* (and *True West*) like for you?

MB: There is no average day. They vary, even from monthly cycle to monthly cycle. Most days include some editing and researching. But I think that kind of variety is good, at least for me. There is no rut to get stuck in. And I learn a great deal from the articles submitted by our contributors. The unveiling of new facts really keeps me going.

EW: Lastly, what words of advice or wisdom would you like to pass on to the next generation of historians and potential editors who may follow in your footsteps?

MB: Be open to possibilities. History is a process, not an end result. New things are discovered all the time. Be skeptical but kind about what's already been written. Be generous with your findings. Be prepared to have your findings questioned—or to possibly be the target of personal attacks. It takes a tough skin to work in this field. But the rewards (not financial) are so great!

Roy B. Young is a noted Earp historian who has written numerous biographies of supporting characters crucial to the Tombstone story. The former president of the Western Outlaw-Lawman History Association (WOLA), Young later helped the merger between WOLA and the National Association for Outlaw and Lawman History to form the Wild West History Association (WWHA). It is within this organization that Young, a resident of Oklahoma, has served as the longtime editor for the WWHA *Journal* until his retirement at the end of 2023.

EW (Erik Wright): It has been a very busy writing season for you lately. Last year, you brought us the incredible *A Wyatt Earp Anthology* (with fellow editors Casey Tefertiller and Gary Roberts, University of North Texas Press) and now you have just completed a book on Newton Earp with another on Billy the Kid on the way. What keeps you focused?

RBY (Roy B. Young): The thrill of the search. I've always loved the process of researching a topic or character. Knowing there is always more to know, I've developed techniques that allow me to keep digging long after others might have stopped. And success in the research process keeps the adrenaline flowing and the motivation at a high level.

EW: Talk about the *Wyatt Earp Anthology*. That book got quite a bit of attention upon its release. How did you come up with the idea for the book and how did you manage to include so many notable historians within its pages?

RBY: Having the Wyatt Earp book named "Book of the Year" by both *True West* and the Wild West History Association was quite an honor resulting in a feeling of satisfaction with our two years plus of concentrated work. I had approached UNT (University of North Texas) Press a number of years ago with the idea and Ron Chrisman, head man at the press, was interested from the beginning. Characters like Billy the Kid, Jesse James, and George Custer already had anthologies, so it seemed natural that another one of America's favorite frontier characters should have his.

One regret was that, even though the book has 63 chapters and 861 pages, we had to cut too many excellent articles to fit the production limitations. There was no intent to omit articles by Neil Carmony, Lee Silva, Steve Gatto, or other fine Earp historians but it became necessary and was a gut-wrenching thing to do.

EW: Is that book the final word on Wyatt Earp?

RBY: No. There will likely never be a "final word" on Wyatt or the Earp brothers. Casey has recently come up with some new information on the Earp family in Kansas. My work on Newton Earp has brought forward some previously unknown and under reported stories that will soon be told.

EW: What got you interested in outlaw and lawman history?

RBY: My interest in outlaw and lawman history really started through a love of genealogy, family history, and constant reading of American history books when I was a teenager. I knew from about the age twelve that Wyatt Earp killed my relative Frank Stilwell and I wanted to know the whole story of the Stilwell family in the Wild West. Additionally, my great grandmother's brother, A.J. Sowell, had written so many books and articles on early Texas history and Texas Rangers that were available to me; I devoured them and now know that I have some 27 blood-related ancestors who were Rangers, perhaps a record number for one person.

EW: You have written extensively about some of the key players of the Tombstone story, but who may not normally receive much attention. Folks like Frank Stilwell and Pete Spence. Who were these guys and what were they really like?

RBY: What many Earp and Cochise County Cowboy War students don't know about Frank is that he was a self-made entrepreneur and successful businessman before the age of 25. He came from a good family, noted by the frontier scout and U.S. deputy marshal Jack Stilwell, but he got into the wrong crowd, turned bad, and suffered the ultimate penalty. Pete Spence, alias of Elliott Larkin Ferguson, even though he was a Texas Ranger for a while, was a low life almost from the beginning and had a major negative influence over Frank Stilwell.

EW: Tell us about your new books on Newton Earp and Billy the Kid.

RBY: The Newton Earp book, virtually complete, came about because of my friendship with some of his direct descendants, especially Bruce and Eric Erdman. Newton was never part of the "Fighting Earps," but was a fine lawman in his own right in Garden City and Finney County, Kansas. His story deserves to be told.

The genesis of the Billy the Kid book goes back to a research assignment I took on for my friend and now co-author, Kurt House. He purchased a pistol that had belonged to one of the two posse leaders who was instrumental in the chase and capture of Billy the Kid and associates culminating at Stinking Spring in December 1880. The posse leader was Frank Stewart, who, with Pat Garrett, received so much acclaim for the Kid's capture. In tracing out Stewart's story we learned that he had been almost completely overshadowed by the Garrett/Upson book and subsequent books and articles through the last 140 years, that we determined to reevaluate the contemporary accounts and documentary evidence to give Frank Stewart his due.

EW: Why has Newton been so overlooked by other writers throughout the years?

RBY: Newton never had a "Gunfight at the OK Corral" experience. He was not one of the "Fighting Earps." After many thrilling adventures in the Civil War, he lived mostly a quiet life as a Kansas lawman. My book on Newton will show another side of the Earp brothers not generally reported, some qualities of which Wyatt had, less the vengeance factor.

EW: You are the longtime editor of the Wild West History Association *Journal*. As someone with the pulse on the current state of western history, where do you see the field going over the next few decades?

RBY: My role as editor of WWHA *Journal* and its predecessor WOLA *Journal* has put me in regular touch with literally hundreds of Wild West historians and aficionados. There are regularly new folks becoming interested in the field, but we need another *Tombstone* movie to catch the attention of a younger generation. I'm thrilled with the current generation of authors and their dedication to producing documented books and articles on the Wild West. The future looks good and the 500 some members of WWHA around the world are leading the way.

Robert K. DeArment was considered by most to be the foremost expert on outlaw/lawman history. A World War II combat veteran, DeArment wrote hundreds of articles and many celebrated books on the subject during his lengthy career. This interview was the last one conducted with DeArment before his passing in 2021.

EW (Erik Wright): What brought you into the field of Western history and writing?

RKD (Robert K. DeArment): As a boy raised in Pennsylvania, I read a lot of western fiction and saw many a western movie and enjoyed it all, but somewhere along the line I began to wonder how much of these stories were based on the history of the West and not just products of some writer's imagination. So, I searched out "factual" books by writers like Burns and Lake and found the "real" stories about actual Westerners fascinating. When I often saw the name Bat Masterson often in these books, I tried to find a biography of the man and was unsuccessful. So, always having an itch to be a writer, I decided I would write Bat's biography. This led to my first book, published in 1979 by University of Oklahoma Press and still in print. I've been running down and writing about lesser-known western characters and events ever since.

EW: Your latest book is titled *Man Hunters of the Old West*. What compelled you to pursue this particular project after years of researching outlaws and lawmen?

RKD: My major interest in western frontier history has been bringing law and order into what was a vast wild country populated to a great extent by wild, unruly men. In my research I had come to know how difficult it was for men who dedicated to protecting their lives and property from the lawless in this vast wilderness and their stories, if ever written, were published many years ago and have been forgotten by the current generation. It's time they were reminded. Selection was easy; there were a lot of these fellows, some wearing a badge and some not. A second volume of Man-Hunters will be coming out early next year.

EW: In your opinion, what are some fundamental truths about the history of the American West that should be retained by future generations?

RKD: I am a proud member of what has been called "The Greatest Generation," the one that survived the Great Depression and banded together to crush two of the most evil regimes in human history that emerged in Germany and Japan in the '30s and '40s. But although my generation stood tall when needed, I am still in awe of the several generations of Americans who in the nineteenth century turned a vast wilderness into what agriculturally came to be called "the Breadbasket of the World" and industrially into what would become the most powerful country in the world. Establishing law and order was part of that great story and all Americans should be proud of the folks who accomplished that amazing feat.

EW: What effect do man hunters as depicted in the book have today's society and modern law enforcement?

RKD: The extraordinary work in law enforcement performed daily by local, county, state, and federal organizations we take for granted today would never have been achieved but for the pioneers in western law enforcement, some of them illiterate, and all unschooled in law and its enforcement. They were as important to the growth and opening of the West as the pathfinders and military heroes.

EW: What are some of the myths that still plague the field of Western history?

RKD: Now you've hit me in a tender spot. For many years I have railed against the major culprits in this ongoing problem, motion pictures and television productions that falsely depict the frontier West and glamorize criminals like the James, Younger and Dalton brothers and even serial murderers like Billy the Kid and John Wesley Hardin, all of whom contributed absolutely nothing to the development of the West but actually deterred that development by stealing from and killing settlers and lawmen. Even shows like Ed O'Reilly's series, Legends and Lies, while claiming to correct some western myths, strengthened others by giving them credence.

EW: As a two-time biographer of frontier lawman, gambler, and journalist Bat Masterson, what do you believe were his last thoughts when he died at his desk in New York City while working for the newspaper?

RKD: I'm a grassroots historian and a writer, not an amateur psychiatrist and have no idea what Bat was thinking. Maybe what he would have for lunch?

EW: What advice can you offer for younger historians looking to pursue a career in this field?

RKD: After digging into this stuff for more than half a century, I am constantly amazed by finding new material that has never really been examined. My only advice to a young entrant into this field is to immerse oneself in the best that has been written and then pick out something those writers have ignored and go after it.

Sandy Barnard is a Vietnam veteran and renowned historian of the frontier military, and he discusses his new book *George Armstrong Custer: A Military Life*. Barnard has written extensively on the military experience in the west with a special focus on Custer and for 23-years served as editor of the annual *Greasy Grass* magazine, a publication dedicated to the study of Custer and the Battle of Little Bighorn.

EW (Erik Wright): Who was George Armstrong Custer?

SB (Sandy Barnard): George Custer must be defined by the era in which he lived. If he lived in the 2020s, he would follow different beliefs as a military man and perform his duties just as his fellow modern officers do. In his time, he was no homicidal maniac, who hated his enemies and would ditch even his friends, if necessary, in combat. He was well-schooled at West Point, despite a poor academic record. On the battlefield, he did not fear combat or death. He looked for opportunities to take charge, even when he was merely a lower-ranking company-grade officer. He impressed his superiors and quickly moved up to staff and command positions that carried greater and greater responsibility. Yes, he could be flamboyant and longed for glory, but an ambitious officer was a rare commodity, especially in the early years of the war, for the Union Army. In the war he became renowned for his enthusiastic cavalry attacks as commander of the Michigan Cavalry Brigade and the Army of the Potomac's Third Cavalry Division. At times, Custer's charges on the battlefield may have appeared challenging, if not reckless, and the young leader's men often sustained high casualties. Nonetheless, Custer contributed mightily to the

Federal victory over the Confederacy between 1861 and 1865.

In modern circles, Custer is less highly thought of because after the Civil War he fought a second war, one that today is viewed more critically by many Americans. Custer, a man of distant 19th century sensibilities, undoubtedly had few qualms about his military actions against American Indians between 1866 and 1876. Although Custer spoke out against tribal mass destruction at times, today, he is often dismissed as an Indian hater and a symbol that is as out of step as Confederate memorials on southern village squares.

Frankly, it is that symbolic and legendary Custer that Americans puzzle over today. The facts of the Civil War, the Plains Indian wars, and Custer's actions and role do not change, although succeeding generations may reinterpret them. At his worst, Custer is forever reckless, courageous, egotistical, ambitious, brash, arrogant, and successful as a fighter. He can never leave that last stand hill on the Montana battleground where a granite monument to him and his men has stood since 1881. Modern military veterans are often offered a handshake and a word of thanks for their service to their country. Custer and his 7th Cavalry troopers are the symbolic exception in American military history. Because they campaigned against Indians under orders from the United States Government, they must roam the plains in disgrace, seemingly forever.

EW: What motivated Custer's military ambitions in the West?

SB: Interesting question, because it presupposes that in his ambition Custer somehow differed significantly from other human beings. He actually was quite similar to most other people who lived in his times as well as modern folks — he wanted success in his life. And, by the time he made his way onto the Plains in 1866, he had already been highly successful. As a major general, he had led thousands of cavalrymen in brilliant charges for the Union Army. He deserved all the praise that was bestowed on him. Of course, at times he appeared immature in his ways, and critics, especially today, somehow think that made him different. The majority of today's young people in their 20s and 30s are highly ambitious and differ little from Custer. Young graduate students aspire to be full professors or presidents of their universities. Young school board or city council members dream about higher office at the state or national level. We just don't like to admit that to ourselves!

EW: Were there any fundamental differences in the Custer of the Civil War versus that of Custer the Indian fighter?

SB: I don't think such differences existed within Custer himself. He was still a brave and fearless warrior. But the combat circumstances on the Plains were entirely different from what Custer had experienced in the Civil War. He may have been too slow to adapt to the new ways of fighting when it came to Indian warriors, but so weren't most of his fellow officers in that period. As a military officer, Custer did not fear meeting his enemy and closing in combat with them.

EW: Let's talk about the Battle of the Little Big Horn. On the day of the battle did Custer have any premonition of what was going to happen?

SB: Some historic descriptions from his officers suggest that Custer seemed "different" that June 25, but no one truly explains how or why that was so. Instead, we follow up by focusing on the outcome of the fighting that occurred that day that cost Custer and hundreds of his soldiers their lives. Many conclude that Custer may have seen the coming disaster. Silly notion! Custer was a very practical, experienced military officer. He did not fear combat, nor did he fear dying in combat. He always expected to win and did not go in for premonitions or other hoodoo.

EW: If it wasn't for the Little Bighorn battle, how would we remember Custer today?

SB: Simply as one more of the great cavalry officers associated with the Union Army's victory against the Confederacy. By the end of the war, the Union was blessed with a large number of such figures. Some battle students attempt to argue that Custer was the best cavalry officer, but I see no purpose in doing that. Indeed, at times he may have been more lucky than good. Often, his comrades spoke of Custer's Luck. Why did he survive the terrible combat of 1861-1865? Simply, because it was never his time to go.

EW: What about the native view of the battle? How is Custer and his legacy thought of today?

SB: The native view today focuses on the idea of what they lost, or what was taken from them. They place little emphasis on the concepts of a changing environment, a developing nation, and an evolving structure of life. Instead, blame is more often placed squarely on multiple generations of greedy, evil white men, such as Custer, who were responsible for such violent actions against their historic people. Today, seldom do they look at the overall complicated human, political, social, and economic motives at work on both sides in the 19th century. As I say in my book, the vast majority of white settlers who moved forward onto the plains came seeking not conquest but a better life for themselves and their families. In that sense they mirrored most immigrants throughout American history, including today.

On the other hand, American Indians were equally mystified by these strangers whose skin, customs, dress, language, and expectations differed markedly from their own. They found little common ground with Europeans who began to carve out new lives for themselves as if they already owned the lands where Indians had lived and roamed for centuries. Of course, Indian responses varied, but sometimes they were provoked into open warfare to maintain their own way of life. More lived peacefully near white settlements.

By the time Custer ventured onto the Southern Great Plains in 1866 and 1867, the Indian population was already enduring severe stress on its traditional nomadic life. For many generations, plains inhabitants had relied highly on a single resource to maintain their lifestyle—the buffalo. By that period, those once vast herds were diminishing rapidly. Technological changes, mostly introduced by the white man, were occurring. Tragically, the Indian had no magical response to all that was going on around him. For the most part their great leaders resorted to warfare against the whites instead of attempting to figure out what the future actually held for their tribal members if they were to continue to exist.

In that last decade of his life, Custer never functioned as dynamically as many of his followers have claimed. Likewise, a single army lieutenant colonel hardly deserves the shameful responsibility for the near demise of American Indians, a process that had been underway hundreds of years before he was born. The clash of cultures that occurred on June 25, 1876, and that ended Custer's life was far more complicated than his own actions in that final battle would suggest.

EW: Your recent book *George Armstrong Custer: A Military Life* looks to dispel many of the myths surrounding the Custer story while offering a concise and readable biography of the man. What prompted you to write the book and what challenges did you encounter while doing so?

SB: In the early 1980s, I began researching the life of news reporter Mark H. Kellogg, who covered the Custer campaign in 1876 for the Bismarck, Dakota Territory *Tribune*, and died with the 7th Cavalry troops on the slopes below the modern Custer National Cemetery on Little Bighorn Battlefield National Monument. To get to Kellogg, I realized I needed to go through Custer, who was the dominant figure for both sides in 1876. My Kellogg biography was to be my first book but ended up by its publication date in 1996 as my fifth. My Custer biography of 2021 proved to be my 17th book. In the intervening years I had gained considerable knowledge about Custer the soldier and Custer the man. So, I was prepared for the task when the South Dakota Historical Society Press asked me to write the Custer biography.

As for challenges, fortunately, it was more time than anything else. I had already written biographies about four other men related to Custer. Each had necessitated that I learn more about Custer. Other books of mine, including my archeology-related titles and my photo histories, gave me great insight into the battle itself. As for the Civil War years, just before I tackled the Custer biography, I had edited the letters of one of Custer's military aides who had served him when he commanded the Michigan Cavalry Brigade in the Civil War. Thus, I began my work on the Custer book already possessing considerable knowledge about the key periods in his life, from his childhood in New Rumley, Ohio, all the way to a lonely outcropping on a ridge about the Little Big Horn River in Montana Territory.

EW: How did Custer's defeat at the Little Bighorn alter military policy on the western frontier?

SB: If anything, the Custer defeat, and the chaotic campaign of 1876 revealed to the army that it needed to take Indian fighting more seriously, but I think change came more slowly and for reasons other than the Little Bighorn. About 15 years ago, I wrote a new introduction for a reprint of *The Old Army*, the memoirs of Major General James Parker. He graduated from West Point in 1876 and served as an army officer throughout the World War I years. During my research of Parker's life and career, I uncovered what amounted to early officer efficiency reports for him. Prior to the Custer battle, such documents were not completed for officers, but in the years afterwards, all the way to today, they are standard ways of assessing an officer's performance. The training for enlisted soldiers changed, too. Prior to the Custer battle, most training occurred at unit level. Ever since, generations of Americans serving in the military have gone through boot camps, before heading to more specialized training. In the aftermath of 1876, the army became more professional.

Patricia Tyson Stroud is the author of several books including *Thomas Say: New World Naturalist*, *The Emperor of Nature: Charles-Lucien Bonaparte and His World*, *The Man Who Had Been King: The American Exile of Napoleon's Brother Joseph*, and, with Robert McCracken Peck, *A Glorious Enterprise: The Academy of Natural Sciences of Philadelphia and the Making of American Science*. Stroud has been recognized with Special Citation for Outstanding Work of Non-Fiction by a Philadelphia Author from The Athenaeum of Philadelphia and in 2001, she was an honoree among the Best Books of the Year for 2000 from the *Library Journal*.

EW (Erik Wright): How did you develop your interest in Meriwether Lewis?

PTS (Patricia Tyson Stroud): My interest in Meriwether Lewis was sparked by the Bicentennial Exhibition of the Expedition held at the Academy of Natural Sciences in

Philadelphia in 2006. The character of the expedition leader came through strongly to me as a fascinating man, courageous, resourceful, knowledgeable, and dedicated to fulfilling his mission.

EW: How did your interest evolve into the new biography *Bitterroot: The Life and Death of Meriwether Lewis*?

PTS: I read a few biographies of Lewis and did not think they captured the man I had encountered in the exhibition, neither in his journal entries from the expedition, nor in certain of his easily accessed letters, particularly in those to Jefferson.

EW: Let's talk about Lewis' death: was it murder or suicide?

PTS: I believe very strongly that it was murder. There is no evidence in his personal letters or those of his friends or enemies that he was alcoholic and depressed and therefore suicidal as most recent writers have claimed.

EW: Lewis was a close and personal friend to Thomas Jefferson. Was this instrumental in Jefferson's decision to send Lewis west?

PTS: I think the fact of Jefferson having known Lewis and his family for much of Lewis's life, both living near Charlottesville, Virginia, in addition to what he learned about him when Lewis served as his secretary during Jefferson's first term as U.S. president, convinced him of Lewis's qualifications for the job.

EW: How was Lewis as a leader of men? Did he and Clark share responsibilities?

PTS: Lewis was a strong and capable leader of men. At the time of his appointment, he had already been in the army for ten years where he had encountered hostile Indians and endured the hardships of wilderness living. Lewis and Clark shared most of the responsibilities except that Clark drew the maps and was the better boatman, while Lewis took celestial calculations and collected and wrote about the natural history specimens found along the way.

EW: Following the expedition down the Missouri River and to the Pacific many believe that Lewis sunk into a deep depression. What evidence is there for this?

PTS: There is no evidence for this. Frederick Bates, Lewis's secretary in St. Louis, disliked him and complained about him constantly in candid letters to his own brother, but not once did he mention depression. Nor is there any mention of it in Clark's letters to his brother, or in Lewis's own letters to friends and relations. The idea of depression stems from several mysterious letters written after he left St. Louis for the East, letters with dubious and unverified credibility that have been seized on as the truth.

EW: In your opinion how important was the Lewis and Clark expedition to the settlement of the American West?

PTS: I think it was very important. It gave the American people an idea of the vast previously unexplored land that lay beyond the Missouri River and the huge mountain range that Jefferson had thought was no higher than the Alleghenies. The expedition made clear that there was no direct water route to the Pacific, but that it was possible to reach the ocean with certain land connections. And it was important to know that there were numerous Indian tribes, but for the most part, with certain diplomacy, it was possible to make friends with them as trading partners.

EW: While Lewis died prematurely not long after the expedition what do you believe he would think of how manifest destiny secured both coasts of the American continent into the 21st century?

PTS: He would undoubtedly be pleased that the United States had become so strong and successful that it reached from one ocean to the other. He was deeply patriotic, proud of his country, and dedicated his life to serving it.

Brooks Blevins is the Noel Boyd professor of Ozarks Studies at Missouri State University in Springfield Missouri. Dr. Blevins has authored several books and many papers on the history of the Ozarks region and has interests in the folk history, education, and religion of the south. His most recent work is a trilogy on the history of the Ozarks published by the University of Illinois Press.

EW (Erik Wright): Your latest work is a three-volume series on the history of the Ozarks of the American Midwest. How did you first become interested in this region?

BB (Brooks Blevins): I grew up on a little farm in the Ozarks and have deep roots in the region. Throughout my childhood I heard the stories of my grandparents (who lived just a quarter mile down our dirt road) and the stories of their brothers and sisters who lived on other farms in our community. So, I was very interested in my own history in the hill country; I just never knew that history had a regional context until I got to college and came across a book on the Ozarks. At that time (the early 1990s) there was very little real history that had been published on the region. A professor who had grown up in New York City and attended Harvard and Stanford convinced me that the history of the Ozarks was indeed a legitimate topic for a senior thesis, and I've been researching and writing about the region ever since.

EW: Where are the Ozarks and who lives there?

BB: The physical Ozark uplift encompasses about 45-50,000 square miles bordered very broadly by the Mississippi and Black rivers on the east, the Missouri River on the north, the Arkansas River on the south, and the Grand River on the west. Roughly ninety percent of the land area is in Missouri and Arkansas, but much of the old Cherokee nation of northeastern Oklahoma is in the Ozarks, as is a tiny sliver of southeastern Kansas. The border of the "cultural Ozarks" is mostly the same as the physical Ozarks, though the farther north and east you go in the physical Ozarks the less likely residents are to identify themselves with the region. Historically, the Ozarks has been one of the more racially homogenous regions in the nation, with whites making up more than ninety percent of the population from antebellum days into the present century. But the prevalence of Latino workers in the poultry processing industry – which is very big in some parts of the Ozarks – has significantly altered demographics in northwestern Arkansas and southwestern

Missouri in recent decades. The region is also a popular tourist and retirement destination, which has brought large numbers of newcomers into the Ozarks from the upper Midwest and the South.

EW: What attracted so many Anglo pioneers to settle the region?

BB: Though some early settlers were attracted by the region's plentiful lead deposits, the primary attraction was lots of available, cheap land, both before and after the Civil War. Most early Ozarks pioneers came from the hilly and mountainous areas of Tennessee, Kentucky, Virginia, and the Carolinas. By the early 1800s those areas were already beginning to fill up. Since westward moving settlers generally preferred to settle new places with a similar terrain and climate, people leaving homes in Appalachia found the ridges and hollows of the Ozarks a comforting and familiar place, even if a more rugged and less fertile place than the Mississippi Valley lowlands they had to cross to get there.

EW: What prompted you to research and write the series?

BB: When I came to Missouri State University in 2008 as the first Noel Boyd Professor of Ozarks Studies, my bread-and-butter class was a course on the history of the Ozarks. But the absence of a published comprehensive history of the entire region presented a challenge. So, I decided to write the history of the region, initially planning a fat single-volume book. I spent about three years doing the research, and when I sat down to write the book, I realized that I had way too much information for a single volume. After a lot of discussion with my editor at the University of Illinois Press, James Engelhardt, we agreed that a trilogy on the history of the Ozarks made sense.

EW: Many Americans and others around the world hold onto myths and misconceptions of the Ozarks and its people. Can you discuss some of these?

BB: Like our kinfolk back in Appalachia, Ozarkers have long been stereotyped as hillbillies or mountaineers. Sometimes the stereotypes are negative – hillbillies can be depicted as lazy, violent, law-breaking, shiftless. But just as often the stereotypes present a more heroic if just as mythical image of Ozarkers – resourceful, authentic, close to the land, nonmaterialistic, neighborly. I expect there are still a lot of people around the country who envision Ozarkers living essentially nineteenth century lives in the backcountry, but aside from the sizable communities of Amish we have in the region nowadays visitors looking for genuine, old-timey hill people are probably going to be disappointed.

EW: What role did the Ozarks region play in the settling of the American West?

BB: The Ozark region was an essential part of the story of western settlement in the days between the Louisiana Purchase in 1803 and the beginning of the Civil War in 1861. During those years it was transformed from a sparsely settled place mostly controlled by the Osage to a region containing only the confined remnants of Native American nations and roughly half-a-million settlers, most of them from the hills and mountains of Appalachia. The region played a key role in many of the most famous western movements of the age. Many of the earliest American pioneers to the Louisiana Purchase were drawn to the river bottoms and prairies of the Ozarks. Most of the paths of the Trail of Tears traversed the Ozarks, and the destination for most Cherokees was on the Ozark plateau of present-day Oklahoma. Though it didn't cross the Ozarks, the Santa Fe Trail had a definite economic impact on the region, to the point that Mexican money was commonly exchanged in the region before the Civil War. Ozarkers played key roles in the gold rush and settling of California in the 1850s; the region especially became a major supplier of livestock, and many large cattle drives were launched from the Ozarks. The Ozarks was also the site of the eastern stretch of the Butterfield Overland Trail that connected Missouri and California.

EW: Throughout your career you have written widely about the Ozarks. What challenges did you face when researching this new three-part history?

BB: The primary challenge for any historian writing about a mostly rural and frontier-like place such as the Ozarks is sparse sources. Historians chronicling seventeenth-century New England generally have more plentiful written historical sources than does someone studying the nineteenth-century Ozarks. But, like Ozarkers have done for generations, you make do with what you have. A more personal challenge for me was trying to find creative new ways to talk about events and issues that I've written about before in other books and articles on Ozarks history. Fortunately, this wasn't as much of an issue in the first two volumes of the trilogy.

EW: How has your work on the region been viewed by locals? Are they engaged in learning about their own history?

BB: From the very beginning of my career as a historian, one of my goals has been to write scholarly history that is also readable and interesting to a general audience. At this stage of my career, I'm fortunate to be in a position where

I can focus more on writing for general readers – many of them people like me who live in the Ozarks or have roots in the region – and I don't spend a lot of time worrying about the reviews of my books by other historians that appear in the scholarly journals. I also devote a lot of time to travelling around the Ozarks giving talks at libraries and museums, visiting with people who are just interested in the history of their region and how it fits into the nation's overall story. And there are a lot of those folks out there. I hear from many of them and enjoy learning about the ways their families fit into the history in my books.

Norman Wayne Brown was a retired and disabled Air Force veteran as well as a retired Texas State Parole Officer. Following retirement, Brown became a full-time Western historian and writer and wrote numerous books and articles including a 2013 biography of John Wesley Hardin. He and his wife Bettie lived near Justiceburg in west Texas. Brown died in 2023.

EW (Erik Wright): Your new book, *Man Hunter in Indian Country: George Redman Tucker, Deputy U.S. Marshal* tells of the true-life exploits of a seasoned and tough lawman. Who was George Tucker?

NWB (Norman Wayne Brown): He was born in Franklin County, Arkansas but he, like many of his Tucker relatives ended up in Texas and Indian Territory to help settle the lawlessness. My wife's grandmother was a niece of George Tucker, and she was part Cherokee and French. She said George was of the same bloodlines. George was a town marshal, a deputy sheriff, deputy US marshal, Chief of Police, and Game Warden during his star-packing career.

EW: What led you to discover his story?

NWB: I first read about him in a novel about the Wyoming Range War and remembered I had him in my wife's family tree. Once I knew he was a distant relative, my wife remembered stories told by her grandmother. I soon had enough information and worked on the project for over ten years.

EW: How was law enforcement different in the Indian Territory versus other parts of the lawless frontier?

NWB: What made things different was the federal laws concerning whites versus Indians and the cultural differences. Indian Territory drew criminals like bees to honey. If an Indian committed a crime against another Indian, then the tribes took care of it. If a white person was involved, the federal courts had jurisdiction. It was against the law to transport, sell or consume alcohol inside Indian Territory. A person in Texas for example, could carry, consume, or sell alcohol and be lawful. But, if that person crossed over into Indian Territory with alcohol, it became a crime with punishment of two years in federal prison. Many Texans never got that straight in their mind.

EW: You write from a remote corner in Garza County, Texas. What challenges as an author and historian have you faced being regionally isolated in this regard?

NWB: Very minor challenges as I see it. I have to say that research is the most important aspect of writing a story.

To tell the story, it should be as truthful as the research will allow. One source doesn't carry much weight as I see it. Two, three, or more sources help to draw a conclusion as to what really happened. A friend once said, "The truth is flawed and never accurate. Each time a story is told or written it is altered until it loses all truth." That's something to ponder about, no doubt. Therefore, original written documentation is of utmost importance. Being I am disabled; I cannot do long distance traveling. But I know how to use the internet to my advantage. There are other folks out there, if one can find them, who have information, photos, documents, etc. and finding the right people is always a stroke of luck.

EW: A previous book of yours, co-authored with Texas historian Chuck Parsons, explored the life and misdeeds of notorious gunman John Wesley Hardin. Describe Hardin's motivations as a frontier fighter.

NWB: Hardin was biased. He didn't like Union soldiers; he didn't like blacks or Mexicans. He didn't like bullies or to be pushed around. Instead of fists, with Wes, it was guns. He didn't hesitate when he pulled a gun to shot someone. Killing probably did not bother him in the least.

EW: Just how dangerous was John Wesley Hardin?

NWB: Very dangerous. His brother Joe once told the district attorney of Comanche, Texas that Wes had killed 38 men, and he would be the next. That district attorney had a great fear of Hardin. Another attorney grew up with him and claimed he was just misunderstood. It is impossible to determine how many men Wes Hardin killed but probably no more than two dozen. Even that, however, is a lot of killing.

EW: Talk about John Wesley Hardin's brothers, including James Gibson "Gip" Hardin who was believed to have died off the coast of Florida. Has your research led you to uncover new facts regarding the Hardin boys?

NWB: Yes. while communicating with a lady who gave me a copy of Gip's death certificate provided a lot more information on the family. Another person contacted me and sent me a photograph of Gip Hardin's two lovely daughters. Also, I learned more about Gip and his brother Jeff who married Creed Taylor's daughter Mary. But I did not uncover any new information on Joseph or Wes. But Gip died on dry land and not in Texas. I just finished an article on Gip and I'm looking for a home for the article.

EW: You have been successful in writing for both periodicals and for book publishers. What keeps you motivated in writing about western history?

NWB: I guess it's mainly because I enjoy the chase and the finds. My wife's cousin, Clancy Carlile was an author and wrote the screenplay for Clint Eastwood's *Honky Tonk Man*. I read two of his books and that was a motivating factor. But the core of it goes back to my teenage years. My high school English teacher told me that she knew I was writing papers for other students but didn't know I was charging twenty-five cents a pop. She said, "You should become a writer someday. You have the gift." I'm not so sure about that, I just like to tell stories.

Michael Wallis is a best-selling author and award-winning reporter as well as historian and biographer of the American West. In 2006, Wallis' distinctive voice was heard as the Sheriff in the Pixar Studio's film *Cars*, and he has authored such books as *Billy the Kid: The Endless Ride*, *David Crockett: The Lion of the West*, and *Route 66: The Mother Road*. Wallis has been inducted into Writers Hall of Fame of America, the Oklahoma Professional Writer's Hall of Fame, the Oklahoma Historians Hall of Fame, the Tulsa Hall of Fame, and was the first inductee into the Oklahoma Route 66 Hall of Fame. Additionally, Wallis has been three times nominated for a Pulitzer Prize and once for a National Book Award. He lives and writes in Tulsa, Oklahoma.

EW (Erik Wright): You have written extensively about the history of the American West as well as more recent features of Westward expansion such as Route 66. How did growing up in the mid-west help to shape your perception of the country?

MW (Michael Wallis). I grew up in Rock Hill, Missouri, in west St. Louis County, just off Manchester Road, the original incarnation of Route 66, and a legendary highway that will always be part of my life.

Like many Missourians, I always looked to the West. Missouri has been called the "Mother of the West" and for good reason. Not only is St. Louis the storied "Gateway to the West," the Pony Express, Oregon Trail, Santa Fe Trail, and California Trail all began in Missouri. In the years after the Civil War, Missouri also produced many of the most legendary outlaws.

Early on I was fortunate to figure out that I wanted to be a writer. I was greatly influenced by my mother and by her mother. Without really knowing it, they introduced me to the art of storytelling. Every afternoon I would sit in my grandmother's rocking chair, and she would make soldier hats for me out of the pages of the *St. Louis Post-Dispatch*. She would supply me with strong tea and Lorna Doones (cookies), and she would just tell me stories about being a little girl coming to this country from Germany and about living in Kansas City in the early 1880s. She remembered the day her brothers ran into the house on July 15, 1881, with news that just the day before in New Mexico Territory Billy the Kid had been killed. She remembered the following spring when they again ran into the house and saying the Ford brothers had just killed Jesse James in St. Joseph, Missouri. Those were the kind of stories she would share, and I was hooked.

EW: Some of your books have ranged in scope to cover the greatest of all the American folk heroes and legends including Davy Crockett, Pretty Boy Floyd, and Billy the Kid. Do you have personal favorite character among those and what legendary figure in American history have you not yet written about?

MW: I carved my own niche as a writer of American history and culture. I am drawn to historic figures that are wrapped up in myth, conjecture, exaggerations, and outright falsehoods. Then I set about to find the truth and present the most accurate account of their lives. I slowly peel back the legend and lies and reveal the authentic and accurate story. Invariably, it is always the best story.

Many of the biographies I have written are about well-known figures that have already been the subject of many books and films. That does not deter me. I consider but most often shun the legendary and seek out the reality. I keep my focus on the line that separates the West of myth and the West of imagination.

To do this I keep in mind my personal mantra — there were some white hats and some black hats but by far most of the hats were gray. And some of them were grayer than others.

EW: Describe your writing process.

MW: I constantly rewrite as I write. And I truly mean constantly. When I finish for the day and I know I'm done, the first thing I do the next morning is go right back to where I started, and I go over it again and I rewrite it. Most of the time I am always reading what I wrote out loud. I want to hear it. I want to hear how it sounds. I want to hear whether it sounds true or not. I write very carefully. Sometimes I have big bursts, but the going can also be slow.

I cherish a quote that is attributed to a lot of people, but I think the main source of this quote was Red Barber. "Yes, writing is easy. You just sit down and open a vein." And that's what it's like for me. Writing is hard. It is hard work. It's not gauged by how much money you make, or even how much you're published. It's what goes on in your heart and soul if that's what you're committed to, day in and day out, year after year.

EW: Your latest book, *The Best Land Under Heaven: The Donner Party in the Age of Manifest Destiny*, explores the ill-fated Donner party against the backdrop of westward expansion in the mid-nineteenth century. Why did you feel another book on the Donner Party was needed?

MW: Not only was another book about the Donner Party needed, but it was also long overdue. Just like the other historic figures I have written about such as Billy the Kid or Crockett, the many individuals and families comprising the Donner Party have predictably been associated with the obvious — the acts of survival cannibalism they had to resort to in order to survive. That is precisely why I stand by my claim that although the survival cannibalism is a critical element of the story, there is so much more that has remained untold such as just who these people were and where they came from and what their lives were like before they ventured West as the foot soldiers of Manifest Destiny.

EW: Describe some of the challenges in researching *The Best Land Under Heaven*. Did you retrace any of the trails used by the Donner Party?

MW: As is the case with every book's creation there was no shortage of challenges. That is a fact of life for all authors. The task of writing about such a large number of people was daunting. During the long and often complex research process I found key individuals to focus on based on their overall impact and importance to the overall story.

The assistance I received from the many descendants of the Donner Party families was enormous. William Springer, a sixth-generation Donner descendant, was especially helpful. Bill was relentless in his efforts to ferret out the true story of his ancestors and the others who accompanied them on their westward trek from Springfield, Illinois to California. His family's collection of documents, correspondence, journals, and other materials helped separate this book from all the others that came before. I am eternally grateful for Bill and his family's candor and commitment to telling the true and unvarnished story.

EW: How did the effects of eating the family dogs and, of course, cannibalism, linger with the surviving members of the Donner Party?

MW: When someone is trapped in the Sierras in twenty feet of snow and has eaten everything possible to consume to ward off starvation, they will do almost anything to stay alive. When a mother sees her children freezing and starving and all the oxen and horses have been eaten, the cattle hides have been boiled to make a wretched broth, marrow has been picked from the animal bones, and mice captured in the huts have been devoured, there is no other choice but to kill and eat beloved family dogs and chew on Ponderosa bark and pine cones with no nutritional value. Finally, those barely hanging on to life turn to the sources of protein buried in the snowbanks — the corpses of those who have already perished. Some of the Donner Party descendants believe they should have started survival cannibalism sooner and more would have lived.

EW: To be fair, you have said that "there's so much more" to the story of the Donner Party and if it hadn't been for cannibalism, the party would have been a footnote to history. Why was the Donner Party so important in the fabric of American history?

MW: As I explain in my book, the fate of this group of people following their dreams highlighted the ambitiousness, folly, and sheer arrogance that marked the great expansionist movement that was called Manifest Destiny. In a way, the party became a microcosm of the United States which, while busily consuming other nations

(Mexico and Indian tribes) that stood in the way of westward migration, had the potential to consume itself. There are lessons to be gleaned from this story to this day.

EW: You have hinted about a forthcoming biography of the "Bandit Queen" Belle Starr. How did you intercept her story?

MW: Presently I am working on a biography of Belle Starr, someone whose true story has really never been properly told. My readers will learn about this colorful and enigmatic woman in a year or two when the book comes out. By the way, she wore a dark gray hat.

Terry Smyth of New South Wales, Australia has brought to our shores a needed and timely study of the gang of Australians known as the Sydney Coves (Sydney Ducks) in his latest book his latest book, *Australian Desperadoes: The Incredible Story of How Australian Gangsters Terrorised California*. He is the author of several other books on Australian history including *Denny Day: The Life and Times of Australia's Greatest Lawman – The Forgotten Hero of the Myall Creek Massacre* and *Australian Confederates: How 42 Australians Joined the Rebel Cause and Fired the Last Shot in the American Civil War*.

EW (Erik Wright): Who were the Sydney Coves?

TS (Terry Smyth): In 1848, in Portsmouth Square, the old heart of San Francisco, the California gold rush began when a merchant named Sam Brannan ran through the square waving a bag of gold dust, yelling 'Gold! Gold from the American River!' And it was there where lynch mobs would later howl for the blood of Australian gangsters terrorizing the town.

In 1851, in Australia, three years after the discovery of gold in California, a prospector lately returned from the California goldfields was riding through central-western New South Wales, when, noting the similarity of the land to the gold-bearing regions of California, he took his pick and pan Into a creek bed and washed out five specks of gold. Thus began the Australian gold rush.

In those few fevered years between 1848 and 1851, thousands of Australians left home for California, hoping to strike it rich on the goldfields. The exodus was not entirely made up of gold-seekers, however. Some had no intention of getting their hands dirty. In San Francisco, they sought to make their fortunes by robbery, mayhem and murder. They called themselves the Sydney Coves - 'cove' being Australian criminal slang for 'man'.

Some 20 ex-colonials formed the core of the Sydney Coves, but they had many collaborators on the fringes of the gang. Some were ex-convicts, convicted of crimes in Britain and Ireland, and sentenced to hard labor in Australia; some were escaped convicts; others were native-born villains. They were distinctive in that many wore broad-brimmed straw hats, and all went about armed to the teeth. Most favored Colt Navy revolvers, although their leader, Long Jim Stuart, preferred a brace of .44 caliber double-barrel pistols.

The law-abiding citizens of San Francisco, who feared and loathed these swaggering colonials, derisively called them the Sydney Ducks, after the plain 'duck cotton' clothing many of them wore. But anyone who dared call a

Cove a Sydney Duck to his face would most likely end up a dead duck.

EW: What type of social environment allowed a gang like the Coves to flourish in Gold Rush-era San Francisco and how was that different from their homes in Australia?

TS: Those were the days when California was the original Wild West, and San Francisco was the capital of the Wild West. Deadwood and Tombstone had nothing on 'Frisco. The rate of homicide on the Californian goldfields was 500 per 100,000, and lynch law was the rule rather than the exception. Even by frontier standards the level of violence and anarchy on the goldfields was excessive, but San Francisco was even worse.

The part of San Francisco where Australians congregated, a three-block area between Telegraph Hill and Portsmouth Square, became known as Sydney Valley or Sydney Town. A no-go zone where Australians ran the brothels, gambling dens, illegal bars, and boarding houses notorious as thieves' kitchens, it was described by Herbert Asbury, author of *The Gangs of New York*, as 'the haunt of the low and vile of every kind'.

Several times, the gang burned the city down. The aim was chaos, and amid the chaos they robbed and looted with apparent impunity, with many of the city's police and judiciary in the pay of the Coves. As the Australian gangsters expanded from arson and street crime to extortion and robbery with violence – hallmarks of organized crime – the *Daily Alta California* newspaper warned:

'There is in this city an organized band of villains who are determined to destroy the city. We are standing as it were upon a mine that any moment may explode, scattering death and destruction.'

At the same time, Long Jim Stuart boasted: 'I have heard hundreds remark here that the day would soon come when this country would be taken by the Sydney people.'

EW: In America, the Sydney Coves Gang is a relatively unknown part of frontier history. Why do you suspect they have largely been ignored?

TS: The vigilantes who fought the Coves were in the end so effective that the gang was all but erased from history. Today, Portsmouth Square, where so many events central to this story occurred, is part of Chinatown, and if you ask the average San Franciscan its historical significance, they'll most likely tell you that a scene from the movie *Dirty Harry* was shot there. As for the notorious 'Sydney Valley' district, history marks it only by its later name – Barbary Coast.

EW: Are the Coves well-known in Australia? How did you first come about their story and set out to write their tale?

TS: Australians, too, are largely unaware of the story of the Coves. This is not unusual in a country that for so many generations sanitized its own history, erasing or revising events that might discomfort the pro-British establishment.

The story of the Sydney Coves owes much to a throwaway remark in a Sydney pub, made by an American friend. For some reason, the conversation turned to the 1854 Eureka Rebellion, a battle between redcoats and rebel miners on the Australian gold fields - and the American, a San Franciscan, mentioned the part played in that rebellion by diggers from California. Then he said, 'We did more for Australia in the gold rush days than Australia did for us.'

'What do you mean? I asked, and he said, 'Did you know that Australian outlaws were the scourge of California, and that they burnt San Francisco to the ground?'

Well, no, I didn't know that, so I decided to find out more.

EW: Your other books focus on Australia's frontier history. How did Australia and America compare in the 19th century and do those legacies still help to maintain a common understanding between the two countries?

TS: In the Australia of the 18th and 19th centuries, American virtues - and vices - were greatly influential on the young country. Both were frontier societies, after all, and thus shared similar challenges. In settling a new land, Australian colonists found more in common with Americans than with Europeans of the Old World.

There were Americans on the fleet that in 1788 brought the first colonists and convicts to Australia. Americans were among the earliest sealers and whalers working off the Australian coast. Americans flocked to Australia during the gold rushes of the 1850s and 1860s, and Americans of the California Revolver Brigade were among the rebels at the 1854 Eureka Rebellion and fought bravely in that battle, later described by Mark Twain as 'a strike for liberty' and 'a victory won by a battle lost', like Lexington and Concord.

When the Australian colonies united to become a nation, in 1901, the new Constitution was based on the

American model, and Australians and Americans have fought as allies in two World Wars, Korea, Vietnam and more recent conflicts.

EW: What other impacts did Aussies – criminal or otherwise – have on the frontier of America?

TS: More than 200 Australians are known to have fought in the American Civil War, on both sides. That number includes a highwayman, Captain Moonlight, and, in 1865, 42 men who joined the Confederate Navy when the rebel raider Shenandoah visited the port of Melbourne. As told in my book *Australian Confederates*, the Shenandoah's Australian gun crew fired the last shot of the war, and their ship was the last to surrender.

One Australian, Morris Farrar, fought with Custer's Fifth Cavalry at the Battle of Little Bighorn. Luckily, he was with Reno's brigade and lived to tell the tale.

Anita Huizar-Hernández is an assistant professor of Border Studies in the Department of Spanish and Portuguese at the University of Arizona. She received her Ph.D. in Literature (Cultural Studies) from the University of California, San Diego where she specialized in Literatures and Cultures of the U.S.-Mexico Borderlands, with an emphasis on Arizona. Her research investigates how narratives, both real and imagined, have shaped the political, economic, and cultural landscape of the Southwestern borderlands in general, and Arizona in particular. Drawing from a diverse array of nineteenth and twentieth century archival materials, her work recovers the underexplored history of race relations in the state and their continued impact on local, regional, and national politics.

EW (Erik Wright): Who was James Addison Reavis?

AHH (Anita Huizar-Hernández): James Addison Reavis was an ex-Confederate soldier, a talented forger, and a larger-than-life con artist behind a scam that would become, in the 1890s, the trial of the century. In the late 1800s, he forged archival documents to make it look like he was the rightful owner of an enormous Spanish land grant that covered most of central Arizona and a sliver of western New Mexico. This attempted heist of twelve million acres of land led to a dramatic trial in Santa Fe and a forgotten legend that is the subject of this book.

EW: Reavis' land scam made international headlines during his time but is now almost entirely forgotten. Why?

AHH: You could chalk up the forgetting of Reavis's scam to the simple passing of time and general lack of historical awareness, but in the book, I argue that something more is at work in this particular case. As I researched Reavis's land scam, I realized that it was not only forgotten but in fact can't be remembered because it highlights unresolved questions about land, narrative, and competing versions of history in the borderlands. In a politically charged climate filled with 'fake news' and 'alternative facts,' Reavis's invented history of a fake land grant and its claimant uncovers a long and winding genealogy of deliberately manipulating and distorting the truth in order to claim ownership of the Southwest.

EW: Just how far did Reavis go in his efforts to work his scam?

AHH: Reavis's extraordinarily ambitious plan reads like the plot of a soap opera. He spent nearly two decades forging archival documents around the world in Spain, Mexico, and the United States to create a paper trail for his fake land grant. He then found a woman of uncertain parentage in California and claimed she was the long-lost heiress to his invented land grant. In order to connect himself with her claim, he then married the woman and sued the federal government for the rights to the land.

EW: What did he look to gain by the land grant if he had been successful?

AHH: Reavis stood to gain ownership of over twelve million acres of extremely valuable land. Even before his claim was validated by the U.S. government, he made millions of dollars selling quitclaim deeds to everyone from individual settlers to railroad and mine companies. If his scheme had been successful, he would have been a very rich man indeed.

EW: To many the southwest border is a clear and defined geographic demarcation. You argue that it is a false line dividing culture, society, and national identity. How has the southwest border helped to shape the history of both the United States and Mexico?

AHH: The southwestern border has played a key role in shaping the history of the United States, Mexico, and tribal nations like the Tohono O'odham whose territory was split between the U.S. and Mexico following the creation of the current border. While the border is a geopolitical dividing line that has been superimposed on land that is otherwise more similar than different, it has nonetheless shaped the cultural, economic, and political trajectory of every group that crosses or is crossed by it.

EW: Who was Sofia Loreto Peralta-Reavis and how was she important to the story?

AHH: Sofia Loreto Peralta-Reavis is my favorite part of the Peralta Land Grant saga, even though her story is tragic. James Reavis claimed she was the long-lost heiress to the Peralta Land Grant. He forged baptismal records and other documents to prove her case and then married her so that he could have access to her claim. Although you could see her as just another of Reavis's victims, her part in his story is also what makes the case interesting. Unlike the forged documents, which were easily dismissed by subject experts, it was harder to determine Peralta-Reavis's identity. Was she Spanish? Was she Native American? How can you determine someone's racial identity in a court of law? The court in fact never answered these questions, saying it was beyond their purview to determine who she really was.

EW: How was Reavis' fraud revealed and what became of him?

AHH: Reavis's fraud was pretty obvious and it's actually shocking that he was so successfully duping people for such a long period of time. For one, the shape of his Spanish land grant was very suspicious. Most Spanish land grants followed natural features like rivers and mountains, but the Peralta Land Grant was a perfect rectangle that just so happened to be located on some of the most valuable land in the territory. The archival documents Reavis presented as evidence were also questionable. Expert witnesses proved that they contained spelling and grammatical errors and lettering made with a steel pen, which didn't exist during the Spanish colonial period, among other inconsistencies. For his crimes Reavis was sentenced to 5 years in the federal penitentiary and ordered to pay a $5000 fine. Sofia Peralta-Reavis later filed for divorce on grounds of nonsupport.

EW: You have also written about other legendary figures in borderlands history including Geronimo and Charles Poston. Talk about your interest in southwest history and the importance of fleshing out the lives of those who made such an impact in the borderlands.

AHH: My background is in literature, and I'm interested in studying how we tell the story of the Southwest. I've written about how Geronimo, Poston, Reavis, and Peralta-Reavis are all part of that story, as are many others whose lives are not recorded in official archives. I do a lot of archival research to find stories that haven't been written about yet, or that haven't been written about in a way that shows all their complexities, especially when it comes to things like race and gender. I also write about the role archives and records play in how we imagine southwest history. I'm especially focused on the nineteenth century because I think it set the parameters for many of the debates that we continue to have today, including who gets to tell the story of this place.

Robert M. Utley, a native of Arkansas, was known as the "Dean of Western Historians." He began his career as a summer park guide at what was Custer Battlefield National Monument (now Little Bighorn Battlefield National Monument). He went on to serve as distinguished career in the National Park Service and was a familiar face to many on television shows such as The Real West. Utley's work inspired a whole generation of historians and many of his books and papers are still considered to be the standard word on the subject. This interview is the last one conducted with Utley before his passing in 2022.

EW (Erik Wright): You have been writing books on the history of the American West for over half a century. What motivates you to keep chasing new subjects?

RMU (Robert M. Utley): My motivation for a lifetime of writing is rooted in ambitions that took root in my late teens. I was a ranger-historian at Custer Battlefield National Monument during my collegiate years. I started the chase then, writing a wholly amateurish pamphlet on the battle. A tourist with whom I confided my ambition put up the money, and at 19 I was an author. The copies all sold, and I was convinced that I wanted to write history. The new subjects I keep chasing are all within the American West. I chased new subjects within that field for three reasons: first, interest to me and lots of prospective readers; second, sufficiency of research material; and third, potential for royalties. I kept talking about how comfortable life would be when "my ship came in." *High Noon in Lincoln* (1987) was supposed to be that ship. It never reached shore.

EW: Your catalog of work is among the most respected in the field. Over your career you have looked to uncover the stories behind such notable individuals as Billy the Kid, George Custer, Sitting Bull, Ned Kelly, and Geronimo. What is your process for selecting a project to research for publication?

RMU: I select a project to research and write about based on the same criteria as set forth above. Since *Sitting Bull*, begun in 1988, an added factor of considerable weight has been the thoughts of my literary agent. He was the late Carl Brandt of what is now Brandt and Hochman. He played a large role in guiding *Sitting Bull*, already in progress when we teamed up, and selecting and guiding the mountain men, the Texas Rangers, Geronimo, and Billy the Kid and Ned Kelly.

EW: Who has been the most enlightening individual to write about?

RMU: The most meaningful, if not enlightening, has to be Custer. I am a historian because Custer teamed up with Errol Flynn to inspire me, at the age of twelve, to become a Custer fanatic. That led to six collegiate summers as a ranger-historian at Custer Battlefield, and ultimately to a career in history. See my *Cavalier in Buckskin: George Armstrong Custer and the Western Military Frontier* and my *Custer and Me: A Historian's Memoir*.

EW: Whose story has proven the most difficult to flesh out?

RMU: Sitting Bull proved the most difficult to capture. Researching and understanding a person from a radically different culture is a daunting undertaking. You must master an entirely different way of life and cast your character within that way of life while rigidly avoiding the taint of your own way of life. As an example, Sitting Bull thrusts his arms in a kettle of boiling water and retrieves a hunk of meat from the bottom. Why would any rational person endure such pain? The biographer must seek the cultural explanation. Multiply that by a lifetime, and the historian's task seems impossible.

EW: Over the course of your career the availability of research has evolved to such a degree much of what was once available only in colleges and libraries is now available on your personal computer with an internet connection. What methods of research would you recommend for younger generations of writers who may only look to the internet for their information?

RMU: The internet is an invaluable research tool for the aspiring historian with computer skills. Almost any subject will have internet material useful in research. Much original source material is being rapidly digitized, and the scholar should seek it out as research progresses. But the scholar should not look solely to the internet. Seek the original material that has not yet been digitized. There is plenty, and much of it will prove indispensable to the project. Newspapers, for example, are valuable. Many can be consulted on the internet, but most cannot. A figure's personal papers are likewise essential. Some are on the internet; most are not. So, the internet should be viewed not as the sole research tool, but as an ancillary tool to expand the research process.

EW: In *The Commanders* (University of Oklahoma Press, 2018) you present an appraisal of selected Civil War generals who helped to shape the American West during the Indian Wars. How did fighting in the American Civil War help to prepare these military officers for a seemingly new type of enemy in the American Indian?

RMU: The Civil War did not prepare these officers for Indian warfare except to give them the rank to function as department commanders. Both the Regular Army rank and file and the Indians confronted the Civil War generals with a mission for which most were not prepared. The Regular Army soldiers were not the motivated volunteers who fought for the Union, and the Indian warriors fought in unorthodox ways with which most of the generals were not familiar. The generals treated in *The Commanders* are all brigadiers, department commanders. The department was the critical layer between division and field and the place where the true measure of a postwar general was revealed. I selected for treatment those who served longest as department commanders.

EW: Some notable figures like George Crook and Nelson Miles are included and your analysis. Admittedly these men are probably most remembered for their contributions in subduing the Apache, but with very different tactical outlooks with Crook being more patient and compassionate and Miles expressing a more aggressive approach. Did the two Union veterans differ in the battlefields of the Civil War, too?

RMU: Crook and Miles brought to Civil War battlefields temperaments similar to those manifested in the postwar West. Crook was more steady and methodical than the mercurial, ambitious Miles. Even so, both performed well in the Civil War. In assessing Miles, moreover, one must bear in mind that he was not a West Pointer like most of the generals, but a Boston store clerk. For all his nasty characteristics, he rose from second lieutenant of volunteers to commanding general of the army.

EW: It had been rumored that your 2012 biography *Geronimo* was to be your last book. Since then, you have published two more books. What is next for "The Old Bison"?

RMU: *Geronimo* was indeed thought by many to be my last book. The thought had some substance because I so badly screwed up the formatting that a reader for the publisher wrote that, despite its faults, *Geronimo* should be published because it was probably the old man's last book. But it wasn't. Three more after Geronimo. There may be still another, but at 88 I don't travel for research purposes, and as noted above I don't believe in relying entirely on the internet. Let the rumor mill do its work while I ponder whether another book is in me, and if so what.

Dan Buck is a renowned expert on the Wild Bunch gang and their time in South America. He has published his findings widely in *Americas*, *South American Explorer*, *Peruvian Times*, *Wild West* magazine, *True West* magazine, the WWHA *Journal*, the English Westerners' *Tally Sheet*, and many others.

EW (Erik Wright): Many people know Butch and Sundance only through film portrayals by Robert Redford and Paul Newman. Who were the *real* outlaws?

DB (Dan Buck): Good question. We don't know much about the inner lives of outlaws, and Cassidy and Sundance are no exceptions. Outlaws led furtive lives more than a century ago, moving around, adopting aliases. Few left diaries. With Cassidy and Sundance, both of whom left home at a young age, what we have are a handful of letters, a few reminiscences from family and friends, and a torrent of yarns from people who barely knew them, if at all.

EW: What first prompted your interest in the study of the outlaw duo?

DB: Complete accident. In reading up for a trip to northern Patagonia in early 1986, Anne Meadows and I learned that Cassidy, Sundance, and Ethel Place had ranched in the region in the early 1900s, so we decided to pay a visit. We interviewed Aladin Sepúlveda, who had been living in the ranch house since not long after the trio had departed and thought that it might make a nice little article. After returning to the United States, we poked around the outlaw history community, and soon got drawn into the bubbling controversy about Cassidy and Sundance's fate.

That no one American writers had seriously investigated and written about their life in South America was an added intrigue. One thing led to another, and here we are, 30 years, many articles, and a book -- Anne's *Digging Up Butch and Sundance* -- later.

EW: Talk about your collaboration with researcher Anne Meadows. How does collaborating with a partner on large-scale projects like this ease the research and writing process?

DB: It's always helpful to have someone in-house, so to speak, to share research burdens, bounce ideas off of, argue with, and catch typos.

EW: Your latest work, *The End of the Road: Butch Cassidy and the Sundance Kid in Bolivia* (English Westerners' Society, 2017) has been called the "[possibly] last word on the demise of Butch Cassidy and the Sundance Kid." Describe the research process in investigating their deaths and any challenges you met in Bolivian archives.

DB: There's no such thing as the last word on any subject. New documents will be found; new questions raised; new perspectives formed. One thing leads to another. Surprises are always around the corner, we hope. Otherwise, what's the point?

   Our research approach in South America was not any different than it was up here. Visit the archives most likely to have pertinent documents, pull up a chair, and start reading. Archivists in Argentina, Chile, and Bolivia, by the way, were uncommonly kind to us.

EW: Why did Butch and Sundance decide to find exile in Bolivia? What type of reception did they meet upon their arrival?

DB: Cassidy and Sundance's lives were defined by trouble and flight. They could not keep away from crime or stay put. Trouble did not find them; they found it. They fled some 6,000 miles to Patagonia to homestead a ranch and within a couple of years were again in scrapes with the law, resulting in their fleeing to Chile and then Bolivia. The pattern repeated itself throughout their lives. If they had gone straight in Patagonia, they could have lived long lives, and their grandchildren would today own a small ranch in a lovely part of Patagonia and be working as fly fishing guides.

In Bolivia, their reception, if any at all, was more muted because they were not ranching among fellow expatriate homesteaders, but working the itinerant lives of mine camp laborers, albeit at an American owned mine. I can only imagine that their work in the Bolivian high Andes was tedious and bone chilling. Plus, Ethel had departed. That must have hurt.

EW: Were any Bolivian authorities ever identified as firing the fatal shots? If so, did they leave behind any written correspondence regarding their experience with the American outlaws?

DB: Both Cassidy and Sundance received multiple wounds in the San Vicente shootout, but whether they died in the affray or committed suicide as it tapered off, is not clear. None of the Bolivian patrol members left an account of the fight, but a local judge conducted an inquest. San

Vicenteños and other locals were interviewed, and a report written. Writer Roger McCord found the report, now called the *Expediente*, in the early 1970s. Following his death in 2016, his family donated it to the American Heritage Center in Wyoming.

EW: What has helped to keep the story of Butch and Sundance alive after all these years?

DB: The popular 1969 movie *Butch Cassidy and the Sundance Kid* seriously kick-started national and international interest in the pair. Before that movie they were better described as regional figures, drawing attention mostly from regional writers. William Goldman's snappy screenplay, popping with memorable lines like "You just keep thinkin' Butch. That's what you're good at" embedded the story in our pop culture. The movie modernized the duo and transcended the Western genre.

Following the movie, the history of the duo been advanced by such writers as Pat Patterson, Donna Ernst, Thom Hatch, and Bill Betenson in the U.S., Jeff Burton and Mike Bell in England, Marcelo Gavirati and Osvaldo Aguirre in Argentina, and Limbert Jeréz Lopez in Bolivia.

EW: Are locals in Bolivia acutely aware of their connections to the outlaws' story?

DB: Bolivians, especially in the region around Tupiza in southern Bolivia are aware of the outlaws' history in their country and its impact on tourism. Just last year, La Paz writer Limbert Jeréz Lopez published an excellent account of the Wild Bunch in Bolivia, *Butch Cassidy y Sundance Kid: Innegable Evidencia*.

EW: You are also known for your tireless efforts in helping to dispel myths and fraudulent information spread about the frontier west. These types of stories have become particularly problematic in recent years in online blogs, webcasts, and social media postings. How do you recommend that people disseminate truth from fact in today's world of instant information?

DB: I'm not sure that things were much different 50 or 100 years ago, when you had yellow journalism, dime novels, and luridly exaggerated Western history magazines. Today myths and fakery travel might travel faster, but by the same token can be debunked faster.

How to separate fact from fiction? Pay attention, be curious, be skeptical, read widely. Don't watch television.

EW: What lingering questions still plague you about the Butch and Sundance story?

DB: What were they thinking?

Robert Watt is a professor and Department of Political Science and International Studies Lecturer at the University of Birmingham in the United Kingdom. He is the world's expert on the Victorio Campaign of the Apache Wars during the 19th-century and has written three books and several papers on the subject.

EW (Erik Wright): Who was Victorio?

RW (Robert Watt): Thank you for inviting me to share my thoughts with your readership. I also very much appreciate that I'm talking to a paper that was founded during the events I am writing about.

There's a very long answer to that question but I think a shorter answer will have to suffice. Victorio was a leader of the Chihenne, Warm Springs, Mimbreno, or Ojo Caliente Apaches who resisted the efforts of the US government through the Department of the Interior and the Office of Indian Affairs to concentrate the Apaches on a single reservation in Arizona Territory. For two years he helped direct efforts to negotiate the return of their reservation at Ojo Caliente, New Mexico. When these efforts failed, he directed a devastating guerrilla war that, combined with the diplomatic efforts of Loco who was leading those Chihenne Apaches who were living on the San Carlo reservation, came very close to succeeding. Victorio turns out to have been an exceptional guerrilla warfare expert in a culture where one would expect to see such experts thrive.

I would argue that Victorio has not been forgotten by history but his legacy as a very successful guerrilla warrior has unfortunately been, so far, assigned to obscurity by history.

EW: You have traveled extensively through the southwest borderlands once known as Apacheria. How did these travels help you to better understand the history of the conflict?

RW: Maps and participant accounts are essential to a historian's understanding of events. But there is no substitute for walking the ground to appreciate the lie of the land. I have almost invariably arrived at the site of a battle, skirmish or ambush with a pre-existing image in my mind's eye of what happened. Almost invariably these assumptions were wrong; the sites looked nothing like the image in my head. I'll give you two examples: one general and one specific.

Generally, I have been quite surprised at how little terrain the Apaches needed to launch devastating close-range ambushes. They often quite deliberately chose to site ambushes just before, or immediately after, terrain which posed a more obvious threat of ambush to their intended targets. The intention would be to catch their enemy's off-guard as they were either watching the more difficult terrain half a mile ahead (and not the Apache warriors concealed fifty yards away) or breathing a sigh of relief after having passed through that dangerous narrow canyon.

A specific example is Tres Castillos. I was invited at the last minute in 2005 by Dan Aranda, who incidentally, needs to be much better known as a very influential historian of the Southwest. It was only wandering over the site was I able to appreciate how lucky the Mexican state troops commander, Joaquin Terrazas, was to catch

Victorio. If he had attacked ten minutes earlier, I think the Apaches would have had time to scatter and reform elsewhere. Had he attacked ten minutes later, the Apaches may have been able to take cover on the northern two hills. These are more defendable than the southern hill where they were trapped. They might have been able to hold off the troops until the warriors sent out to replenish their ammunitions stocks returned. I had read all the reports I could find. I also looked at the photographs in Dan Thrapp's book, but it was only seeing the site in three dimensions which allowed me to reach this conclusion.

EW: When most people hear of the "Apache Wars" their imaginations are at once drawn to Chiricahua war leader and medicine man Geronimo. How does the Victorio Campaign fit into the larger context?

RW: The Victorio War fits into the larger context of the Apache wars in two ways.

First it was the most intensive segment of the later Apache wars (1876-1886). If we take the Apache Wars with the US as broadly 1860 -1886, Victorio and Nana's warriors were, in two years, responsible for inflicting 22% of the US troops killed by Apaches between 1860 and 1886. To put this in context, they killed forty-three US troops (not including nine Indian scouts) during these two years. This I think has been conveniently forgotten that the US army failed to defeat the Chihenne Apache resistance to the concentration policy between 1879 and 1881. The survivors of Victorio's resistance did not surrender till 1883 during General Crook's expedition into the Sierra Madre. The Apaches did not win their war for the return of their reservation, but the US army failed to either destroy them or force them to accept the reservation at San Carlos between 1879 and 1881.

Second, the Victorio War was the last time that Apaches tried to fight to maintain control of their land in the USA. After the end of Nana's Raid in 1881, the Chiricahua Apaches, who continued to resist, based themselves in the Sierra Madre Mountains in Mexico only periodically raiding into the USA in search of ammunition.

EW: You research and write from the United Kingdom where you are a lecturer of Political Science and International Studies at the University of Birmingham. Describe the challenges of undertaking a project of this size while living in a different country?

RW: The primary challenge is cost. I've self-funded three quarters of my trips to the USA from 2003 onwards. While the costs are a challenge, I realized quite early on that I was on to something far beyond an interesting historical project. Any cost has been more than offset by fascinating trips to the archives and thrilling field trips to the Southwest. This has allowed me to build up a very large archive of photos of the sites which I hope future historians may find of some utility.

On the US side of the Atlantic I have encountered individuals who are mystified, even hostile, to a British person having the effrontery to delve into US history. On the upside I have encountered far more Americans who have helped and encouraged me along the trail for almost 20 years and they continue to do so.

On the British side of the Atlantic I have been regularly challenged, with the same mixture of mystification through to hostility as to why I would choose to study such an obscure or irrelevant period of history. Again, I have received steadfast support for my project from many colleagues from the start of my research.

The overall answer to this question is that there have been serious challenges, but none have proved to be insurmountable. This is a result of my personal determination to see this project through to the finish but, more importantly, due to the immense support and encouragement I've had from people on both sides of the Atlantic.

EW: What attracted you to the story of Victorio?

RW: Watching 'The High Chaparral' as a child really grabbed my imagination concerning the Apache Wars. My mother is a retired history teacher, and she made every effort to foster any interest I showed in history. My late father was a maths teacher who loved history. He let me stay up to watch a film called 'Hondo' and I saw Michael Pate playing a truly tough and imposing Apache called, if I remember correctly 'Vittorio', who was also thoroughly honorable thus making him a great leader. One of the books I read at quite a young age was 'Bury my Heart at Wounded Knee' where a quite different Victorio briefly appeared. Thus, for about fifteen years, I wanted to know more about Victorio. While I was an undergraduate at the University of Paisley in my mid-twenties I came across Stout's 'Apache Lightning' and a short time later Thrapp's 'Conquest of Apacheria' and 'Victorio'. This led me onto a number of secondary sources concerning the Apache Wars, but they still did not answer most of my questions. It was widely said that Victorio was a military genius. Yet, beyond the fact that he appeared to survive for over a year against large numbers of US and Mexican forces before being killed at Tres Castillos, nobody could tell me exactly why he was such a successful war leader. I finally decided that it was down to me to answer my own question. That was in 2000 and the rest is, as they say, history.

EW: It is widely known, at least among historians of the Apache Wars, that gathering information from living descendants of Apache leaders and prisoners of war is a monumental challenge. Did you manage to overcome these cultural misunderstandings when writing your book?

RW: The work of Opler, Goodwin and particularly Eve Ball in collecting as much information as they could has proved invaluable to my research.

It was an almost throwaway comment by James Kaywaykla from *In the Days of Victorio* which triggered my investigation of Victorio targeting horses during ambushes. I knew that the US army regiments kept a monthly record which included horse records (serviceable, unserviceable, and lost). Each company within a regiment also recorded serviceable and unserviceable horse numbers in their bi-monthly muster rolls. I investigated whether these records would corroborate this claim. You can see the results as the three volumes on the Victorio Campaign unfold. In the financial year July 1879-June 1880, the Ninth Cavalry sustained 34% of the entire horse losses of the US army. From these records I can directly attribute at least three quarters of the Ninth Cavalry's losses to direct (shot during ambushes) and indirect (being led for weeks over difficult terrain) action by the Apaches. The army records also revealed a cumulative effect of increasing numbers of unserviceable horses to the extent that, by the beginning of the summer of 1880, the Ninth Cavalry was temporarily rendered unfit for field service. I'm convinced that I would not have investigated this issue without the material collected by Eve Ball.

I have found that some of the Apache testimony can also be matched up to army reports, newspaper reports and memoirs from this period. This work accomplished before the surviving participants passed away has proved priceless to researchers, such as me born in 1966, who are unable, through the passage of time, to interview participants.

EW: Prior to your work on Victorio you published two books on the Apache as borderlands soldier with specific attention given to their tactics and strategies. How did the Apache way of fighting differ from that of the U.S. and Mexican armies and what elements led to being an advantage which ultimately prolonged the various Apache campaigns for decades?

RW: The Apaches did not assume that their enemies were 'ignorant savages'. They watched their enemies closely and for prolonged periods to pinpoint both their strengths and weaknesses and adapted their own strategies and tactics to minimize the effect of the former and to maximize their effect upon the latter.

Recent archaeology, carried out by Karl Laumbach, has shown strong evidence that the Apaches appreciated the technical strengths and weaknesses of various types of breech-loading and repeating rifles/carbines and tried to deploy to maximize the advantages of the various effective ranges of such weapons in their deployments at the battle of Hembrillo Canyon in April 1880.

They also realized that the Telegraph lines could be turned to their advantage. By tearing up a quarter of a mile of telegraph line, they could tempt the army into fruitless horse-killing pursuits. If they wanted to delay the army's deployment, they would cut the line and then reattach the lines. This would force the repair teams to check every pole to find and repair the break.

The Apaches' most dangerous opponents were those individuals who saw beyond the 'ignorant savage' assumption and tried to understand the thinking of the Apaches. I hope that one of my key contributions to the history of the Apache Wars is to outline just how sophisticated were the tactics and strategies used by the Apaches during the Victorio War. My research has argued that even where Victorio was defeated by Grierson in Western Texas and when he was killed at Tres Castillos, he was using strategies and tactics which came very close to winning in both cases. In both cases he was faced by commanders, Grierson and Terrazas, who did not underestimate the Apaches.

Garner A. Palenske wrote, *Wyatt Earp in San Diego, Life After Tombstone* which was published by Graphic Publishers. This work was the first academic treatment of this important period of Wyatt Earp's life. Since then, he has been published in the WWHA *Journal*, *True West* magazine, and other publications. Garner is a member of the WWHA, the San Diego History Center, and serves as the President of the Broad of Directors for the Courthouse Museum in Old Town San Diego.

EW (Erik Wright): How did your interest in the American West evolve?

GP (Garner Palenske): I was surrounded with Western historical influence most of my young life, I can credit my father with that. My father's family were German immigrants who settled on the Kansas frontier. As a child my father repeatedly talked about this and showed me newspaper articles about our family during that period. Our family vacations were usually spent in Mexico where I learned to ride horses. In the winter we visited the Mojave Desert where my father taught my brother and I to shoot a 19th century single barrel, breech load shotgun his grandfather learned to hunt with. My favorite adventures were the trips we made to the ghost towns of the Mojave Desert. Even at a young age I pondered the romance and intrigue of the miners, lawmen, and outlaws who lived in these desolate towns.

EW: Specifically, how did you become interested in Wyatt Earp and Tombstone?

GP: We were planning a family vacation to Hawaii, and I was looking for a book to read on the flight. I randomly found a book about Wyatt's time in San Diego, written by Ken Clich. I visited Ken in the Wyatt Earp Gaslamp

Museum he owned. That meeting further stimulated my Wyatt Earp interest. After that trip I started reading all the volumes about Wyatt I could find. It was surprising to find many books contained the same situation, but with different details or outcome. Also, Wyatt was portrayed as a hero in some books, and a villain in others. At this point in my life, I thought all history books were accurate and I was confused by the dichotomy of the stories. My wife suggested that we visit Tombstone, home of that famous historian Ben Traywick. Ben certainly could straighten this out, she thought.

That first trip to Tombstone was magic. I spent three hours with Ben talking Earp. Finally, he got tired of talking to me and excused himself. We said goodbye and as I walked off the boardwalk on 5th Street towards the *Epitaph* Newspaper Museum, something told me to look back at Ben's office. I turned around, and through a small window saw Ben sitting at his desk reading something or other. At that moment I knew the study of Wyatt Earp history was my direction. I had read about Wyatt living in San Diego and decided to start researching his activities. My job as an engineer includes conducting and publishing research, so I had a good handle on research techniques and a lot of experience writing. And so, the adventure started.

EW: Talk about how your book *Wyatt Earp in San Diego, Life After Tombstone* was developed?

GP: The work began with a literature search of related books, articles, and any research published regarding Wyatt's time in San Diego. The locations of other information sources were identified including the Huntington Library, the Arizona State Archives, the

University of Arizona, the Arizona Historical Society, the San Diego History Center, and various other local historical societies. Digital sources were exploding at this time which increased the efficiency of the research effort. The research portion of the project, which included many trips to these various institutions, was definitely the most exciting and enjoyable portion of the entire endeavor.

I met famous historian Lee Silva in Tombstone at the Helldorado celebration while in the early phases of the project. Lee introduced me to his publisher, Jeff Millet of Graphic Publishers. I was really impressed by the stunning photographs and graphics of Lee's books, so Graphic Publishers was selected for the production. A comparison of Wyatt in San Diego and Lee's Earp books reveals the similarities.

The writing of the book followed the classic engineering project design sequence. The book was broken down into completion milestones; 25%, 50%, 75%, 100%, final draft, and final manuscript. For motivation, the reward for completing each milestone was a weekend trip to Tombstone. These trips included Ben Traywick's review of the manuscript and led to the development of friendships with many of the Tombstone's population. To date, I have visited Tombstone approximately 31 times. In all it took 5 years to finish the book. I estimate it involved at least 3,000 hours of my time.

EW: Describe Wyatt and Josie's time in San Diego.

GP: The time Wyatt and Josie lived in San Diego, 1886-1890, was one of the best of their lives. Wyatt raced horses, ran 3 gambling rooms, and invested in property. Unlike their later life, the Earps were financially solid during this period. They made many friends in San Diego, some of which became lifetime relationships.

There were troubles, however. Gambling was illegal in San Diego and despite colluding with the Police Department, Wyatt was forced to testify in public hearings regarding his shenanigans. No charges were filed, however the public opinion of Wyatt likely suffered. San Diego was the start of Wyatt's horse racing years, and the excitement that followed.

EW: You have often publicly credited Tombstone and western historians Ben Traywick, Don Chaput, and the late Lee Silva with nurturing your interest in Earp and Tombstone. What advice have these men given you over the years as an author and researcher?

GP: "Use primary source research and don't just regurgitate someone else's work. If you don't have any new information, why write a book?" - Ben Traywick

"Wyatt Earp's many friends are a testament to the type of man he was." - Lee Silva

"There is much more to the story of the Tombstone than the Fremont Street Gun Battle."
- Don Chaput

EW: Tell readers about your research and writing process.

GP: I have been educated and trained, both in undergraduate and most recently in graduate school, in the use of scientific methods. I use this approach for historical research as well. Scientific method is defined as a process of collecting data, analyzing the data, developing a hypothesis, and testing the hypothesis to arrive at a conclusion. It may sound complex, but it really is just a method of organizing your thoughts and actions in a logical manner. It's very powerful, especially when you test your hypothesis.

I prescribe to the art of "writing is rewriting" mantra. I constantly reread and revise the narrative as it develops. This probably is not the most efficient method, but it works for me.

EW: What projects are you currently working on for publication?

GP: Now that I have finished graduate school, I'm looking forward to digging deep into research. Since writing the Wyatt in San Diego book I have been researching other under reported times in Earp's life. His adventures at the Harqua Hala, which is located near Salome, Arizona, are an example. Along with Wyatt there were many of the boomtown crowd including Nellie Cashman, Justice Jim Burnett, and John Sevenoaks. I have found Wyatt's mining claim documents and likely the location of one of the claims. A portion of this work was published in *A Wyatt Earp Anthology: Long May His Story Be Told*, by University of North Texas Press. However, there is much more information to publish.

Wyatt's doings in Yuma are another topic of interest. A portion of this can be found in my *True West* magazine article titled *The Fix*.

I'm really drawn to the macro level of the so-called Cochise County War and its effect on the settlement of Arizona. This is a very interesting topic which involves the President of the United States, big business, and Wyatt Earp. Work on this is anticipated.

EW: As the field of western history moves forward to new and younger generations what advice would you like to pass along to future historians who may look to your work in their own research?

GP: The foundation of every good history book is solid research. Never compromise on the research portion of your book project. Just like a building, an inadequate foundation leads to failure. The biggest compliment you can receive is acknowledgment from another researcher that your work somehow helped their research.

Bob Boze Bell: artist, author, historian, publisher. His tenure as Executive Editor at *True West* magazine since the mid-1990s has helped to revitalize the field. With his humor and unique ability to breathe new life into dusty stories through his art and *Life and Times* of books, "Boze" as he is affectionately known is a giant in the field.

EW (Erik Wright): The name Bob Boze Bell has become synonymous with Western history, pop culture, and folklore. What brought you into the field?

BBB (Bob Boze Bell): My mother's mother, Louise Robinson Guess Swafford, known as "Guessie," was from a ranching family in the Bootheel of New Mexico, and she regaled me with stories of our outlaw kin when I was growing up in Kingman, Arizona. According to her we were related to "Big Foot" Wallace, John Wesley Hardin, and Blackjack Ketchum. My mom hated this and was embarrassed by the connection, so that inflamed my interest even more. Then when Grandmother Guessie claimed that my favorite TV show, "The Life & Legend of Wyatt Earp" was bunk, and that "Wyatt Earp was the biggest jerk who ever walked the West," I was flat hooked for life.

Grandma Guessie lived for a while in Rodeo, New Mexico which is not that far from Tombstone. She was there about twenty years after the so-called O.K. Corral fight and all her neighbors were cowboys, so you can imagine why she thought Wyatt Earp was a jerk. In fact, one of the funny things about Cochise County is that in Tombstone proper there is a reverence for Wyatt Earp (he pays a lot of mortgages) but step out into the countryside and you'll get a different take on those Iowa boys.

EW: It has been 25 years since you first published your seminal book *The Illustrated Life and Times of Billy the Kid*. The book gave rise to two other similar volumes on Doc Holliday and Wyatt Earp. Why a book on Wild Bill Hickok and why now?

BBB: My wonderful wife Kathy is a therapist. She claims I am ADD and OCD. Everything has to be perfect, just not for very long. I started doing these big, colorful, illustrated books back in 1992, did three of them, with *Geronimo* and *Wild Bill* on deck, but then I got distracted, landed on a morning drive radio show, started appearing in TV documentaries, bought a magazine and started losing $30,000 a month. As my therapist will attest, I'm easily distracted. Anyway, I woke up 22 years later and thought to myself, "I need to finish that Wild Bill book." So, I did.

EW: Was Hickok's killing of Davis Tutt in 1865 Springfield a lucky shot or pure skill?

BBB: If you've ever fired a pistol, as opposed to a rifle, you know that accuracy is very difficult beyond, say 10 feet. I have a hunch it was a lucky shot, but by all accounts, Hickok was a master marksman, so perhaps he combined both skill and luck. Either way, it's a legendary shot and is the benchmark of Wild Bill's fame.

EW: Jack McCall is still a mysterious figure in the legend and lore of the Hickok story. What is your take on the assassin?

BBB: A total Jackass—in a long line of Jackasses, from Mark David Chapman to that coward on the 34th floor of Mandalay Bay.

EW: In August 2000 you wrote, "I was sitting in class in Kingman wondering how I could get published in my favorite magazine: *True West*. Now I own it!" What have been some of the biggest challenges you have faced during your tenure at *True West* while working tirelessly to revive America's interest in the Old West?

BBB: When we bought the magazine in 1999, I thought it would be a fun gig and everyone would love me for saving a cherished publication. But as soon as I changed the paper stock—*True West* was still being published on pulp paper—the complaints started coming in: "Joe Small is spinning in his grave!" Joe was the founder of the magazine, and I took the criticism to heart. Wish I had a dollar for every time someone said to me, "If it ain't broke, don't fix it." Well, it was broke and we were going out of business in a hurry. The other thing I got a lot of grief over is running articles about Western movies. "Why don't you change the name of the magazine to Reel West." Everyone thinks they are being so clever. I want to say, "Gee, that's the first time I've heard that one, TODAY!" I finally went back and looked at the early issues and Joe was doing articles on rodeo, movies, recipes, all kinds of pop culture stuff and he was selling 250,000 issues on the newsstand every issue. But here's the deal: *True West* was not a history magazine; it was a Popular History magazine. There's a big difference. By the 1970s, when Joe sold the mag, it had gone down to less than 10,000. When I interviewed Elizabeth Small, Joe's wife, I asked her what happened and she said, "The footnote crowd took over."

EW: Hickok was briefly a showman for Buffalo Bill and was known to have a sense of humor when talking to reporters and dime novel writers. What do you think Wild Bill's review of your book would say?

BBB: "Pretty near all these stories are true," which is an actual Hickok quote is one we can all live by. If legend is embellished with facts to make a better story, then historians have the dubious honor of ruining many a good story. My goal is to tell good stories and then tell you how much of it is actually true. All I've ever wanted is to know the truth. I guess you can blame my grandmother for that obsession.

EW: You are known for your intense fascination of many western characters such as Billy the Kid, Wyatt Earp, and the Apache captive turned scout Mickey Free. What figure of the past would you most like to sit down with and why? What burning question would you ask that person?

BBB: I'd love to sit down with Ike Clanton and the McLaurys and say, "Okay, who was actually armed and what the hell did you THINK was going to happen?"

EW: As the field of Western history moves forcefully into the twenty-first century what legacy do you hope to leave behind to those younger generations who look to follow in your footsteps?

BBB: Hopefully I can provoke some snot-nosed kid to try and prove me wrong and keep the flame burning. People mistakenly believe that history is solid rock, but I have learned that nothing changes more than the past. Don't believe me? Okay, prove it.

Gary L. Roberts sold his first article as a student in high school with *True West* magazine; a parallel path that the editor of this volume took. Since his high school days, however, Roberts earned his Ph.D. and rose to prominence as the leading expert Doc Holliday, Western violence, and gunfighter historiography.

EW (Erik Wright): You published your first article in *True West* magazine while you were a student in high school.

Talk about that time in your life and how you became interested enough in western history to pursue such an endeavor?

GLR (Gary L. Roberts): Actually, I sold the article as a senior in high school, and it was published during my freshman year in college. I grew up in the days of Saturday afternoon westerns, and at an early age I was curious about what really happened. I never liked the Roy Rogers-Gene Autry singing cowboy genre, and I guess that contributed to my favoring cowboy stars like Wild Bill Elliott. They seemed more real. I had a grandmother who encouraged my interest in history, shared family documents, photos, and letters dating back to the Civil War when I was still five or six. I was fascinated. By the time I was thirteen, I was reading everything I could get my hands on about the West. In the eighth grade, I wrote a history of the Indian Wars of the West in long hand, replete with footnotes, maps, and illustrations. Regrettably, when I graduated from college, I tossed it out along with other "childish things," but I didn't lose interest in the West. By the mid-fifties the heyday of TV Westerns had arrived, and I had more questions about what was real. I discovered *True West* magazine and the Westerners, along with Frontier Books, W. M. Morrison Book Dealers, and Guidon Books. I was collecting books (south Georgia libraries didn't have many items that helped), and I began to write to every person and historical society that I could think of. It was amazing how many people responded. I learned about Wyatt Earp from the TV show, but I wanted to know more. About 1955, I ran across Walter Noble Burns' *Tombstone: An Illiad of the Southwest.* I was mesmerized by the book and wanted to know more. Not long after that, I ran across an essay,

"Wyatt Earp: Man vs. Myth," written by William MacLeod Raine, who painted a much darker picture of Earp. At that point, I decided I was going to find out the "truth." I increased my research efforts, eventually contacting the National Archives. I asked about Wyatt Earp's service as a deputy U. S. Marshal and eventually received the information that formed the basis for my first article, "Was Wyatt Earp Really a Deputy U. S. Marshal."

EW: How did your career evolve from there?

GLR: Needless to say, publishing that article inspired me. I was a corresponding member of several Westerners groups by then, and I was throwing a wider loop in my correspondence. I published a series of articles in various Westerners publications on Clay Allison and Dodge City, "The Cow-Boy Scourge" (using additional information I had obtained from the National Archives, a biographical article on Newton Earp, and another article in which I raised questions about the problems that historians had with Wyatt Earp. By then, I was in college, majoring in history, and corresponding with a growing list of writers and researchers that included J. Frank Dobie, Ramon F. Adams, Joseph W. Snell, Nyle H. Miller, Allen Erwin, George Washington Earp, Zoe A. Tilghman, Tom Bailey, Harry Sinclair Drago, Joseph G. Rosa, Frank Waters, William R. Cox, Ed Bartholomew, Colin W. Rickards, Robert N. Mullin, John D. Gilchriese, Chris Penn, Charles Leland Sonnichsen, and more. One of them, Harry Sinclair Drago, even took me to task in the New York Westerners *Brand Book* for the radical idea that there might be an alternative to both hero worship and debunkery. At the same time, I was working on my degree in history, and had been introduced to a more academic approach, I took a particular interest in historical methodology and historiography. I found that academics, as a group, had some disdain for gunfighter history, while many popular writers and what we call "grassroots historians" were suspicious of academics. I didn't understand that. I was convinced that the gunfighter was a legitimate subject for history, and non-academics could profit from more academic methods. I determined to write sound, readable "Wild West history" employing rigorous historical methods. I was also continuing my interest in the Indian wars, as the result of my interest in the Sand Creek Massacre of 1864. I completed my M. A. in history in 1967 and began my teaching career. I expected to teach for a year or so and then complete my Ph. D. in history, but events conspired to delay my return to academic study until 1977. I continued to write articles, and to enlarge my circle of correspondents to include Glenn G. Boyer, Robert A. DeArment, William B. Shillingberg, Jeff Morey, Susan McKey Thomas, and others. In 1971, I received the Vivian A. Paladin Award for the best article appearing in *Montana, The Magazine of Western History,* for "The Shame of Little Wolf," an article about Little Wolf, the Northern Cheyenne chief and bearer of the Sacred Bundle of Sweet Medicine. I wrote a variety of other articles on a variety of Western topics including a lengthy piece on Billy Brooks for the Kansas Westerners, a two-part article for *The American West* on the historiography of "The West's Gunmen," and an essay on "Violence and the Frontier Tradition."

EW: Most readers probably know you from your monumental biography on Doc Holliday [**details here**]. However, you have also written a book on political violence in New Mexico as well as a recent study on the 1864 Sand Creek Massacre. What drives your research interests in the history of the west alive?

GLR: In some sense, I guess I never grew up. Those Saturday afternoon Westerns and the Western novels I read as a boy were all tied to violence, but I realized they were fictional. And I wanted to know the truth even then. As I pursued my academic study, I gained a broader perspective, and I gradually came to see myself as a student of frontier violence rather than as a gunfighter historian or a chronicler of the Indian wars. At the center of it all was a need to know if the stories were true and if they were, what explained the violence. This led me years ago to explore the subject of violence in American history broadly speaking as a context for studying violence in the West. My interests coincided with a renewed interest in America's violent past during the late 1960s that led to a federal commission of violence. I've kept that interest alive ever since, especially as it became more popular to discount the volume of Western violence among academics. Now, it is true that personal violence was not at the ridiculous levels of the "Rambo goes west" imagery the movie *Tombstone* devolved into. But it is certainly true that the "no duty to retreat beyond the air at your back" doctrine was well established in fact as well as in law. What has kept my interest alive has been this debate, and studying events like the "Hell-on-Wheels" towns of the Union Pacific (and Tom Smith), the Kansas cattle town experience, the sporting world in the West, the political violence in territorial New Mexico, and, of course, individuals like Wyatt and Doc, not to mention the violence of the Indian wars within the broader frame of "the search for order," to borrow the title of Robert Weibe's history of the Gilded Age. The study of Western violence continues to be timely in light of current debates over contemporary violence and gun legislation.

EW: As the recognized authority on frontier violence can you discuss what gunplay was really like on the frontier?

GLR: First, I would like to point out that the period between 1860 and 1900 was probably the most violent era in American history. It began with the Civil War and the millions who died in that conflict and a surviving generation that came of age with firearms in their hands and human targets before them. Remember too, that three presidents were assassinated between 1865 and 1901, as well as multiple other office holders. It was the era of the last Indian wars fought on the Great Plains and in the Southwest. It was the era of lynch law, especially in the South and West. It was the age of range wars. Nor was violence just a frontier phenomenon. The Gilded Age saw increased labor violence, urban crime rates, organized crime, feuds, county seat wars, and increased racial violence. The engine of this increased violence was industrialization. It manifested itself in different ways. One of the rushes westward, increased in rate by the railroad and the Homestead Act. In the West, with the railroad's westward push settlement pushed beyond government and law and community and family into a volatile environment of "Hell-on-Wheels" towns, cowtowns, mining camps, and other boom environments where men frequently resolved their differences personally and with gunplay. In the East, industrialization introduced massive numbers of industrial workers into the cities and disrupted the existing sense of community. There too, ethnic conflict increased. In the South, in addition to racial violence, "shoot on sight" duels became commonplace, a variant on Western gunfights and a more "modern" and populist variant of the code duello of the Old South. A key component of the gunplay was the development of repeating rifles and revolving pistols. Homicides and other violent crimes were more numerous than other places because of the social conditions and subsided over time as legal forms and community standards took over. Of course, the ritual of gunfights we saw in the movies was more myth than reality and "fast draw" played a lesser role than we might have imagined after watching Matt Dillon for twenty years, but personal gunfights were a part of the Western scene for several decades. Curiously, the very term "gunfighter" came into common use in the late 1880s, almost as the result of a need for a term to describe a type that was even then passing from the scene. The sporting scene, liquor, prostitution, and exaggerated notions of personal honor all played their roles in feeding the phenomenon. I haven't seen much of the stereotype of young guns traveling from place to place looking for better known gunhands to challenge in order to build a reputation as a gunfighter. But beyond doubt there were men who were regarded as "pistoleers," "bad men to tangle with," and dead shots ready to kill. The model for the "image" of the gunfighter was clearly Wild Bill Hickok. And WWHA members can certainly make lengthy lists of gunfights which suggests almost an ethos on the subject. More than that, in the decades between 1880 and 1910, the gunfighter was romanticized nostalgically until by the 1920s the gunfight carried an even greater weight as myth than as history. What is often underplayed is the extent to which lesser forms of violence played the greater role in the boom camp environments. The "bad man for breakfast" stereotype marked a particular phase of boom town development. There were more homicides by firearms in the first year of Dodge City's existence than for most of its cowtown history combined. Order was in the interest of towns like Dodge and Tombstone and Virginia City.

EW: The recent book, *A Wyatt Earp Anthology: Long May His Story Be Told,* was recognized in January by *True West* magazine as the non-fiction Book of the Year. As an editor of that book and lifelong student of Earp what have you come to learn about a man shrouded in myth and misconceptions?

GLR: If you read the description of Wyatt Earp in Chapter XV, "The Out Trail," in Walter Noble Burns's *Tombstone*, Bat Masterson's defense of his friend in *Human Life*, and the concluding paragraph of William McLeod Raine's essay, "Wyatt Earp: Man versus Myth" (which appears in the *Anthology*), you'll gain a pretty good sense of where I started my quest to understand Wyatt Earp. I didn't read Stuart Lake until later, and I had some problems with his book from the start, but I found the debunkers like Waters and Bartholomew dissatisfying. In fact, for most of the years that I have studied Earp, I have been frustrated by the determination of many, if not most, writers to portray him either as a frontier hero or as a thug. At one point, back in the seventies, I packed up my Earp materials in frustration over the state of the field and determined to pursue other interests. I corresponded with a few old friends and answered questions when asked by some new ones, but the field seemed to me somehow tainted. Inevitably, however, I was drawn back to the field, almost had to be once I renewed my interest in Doc Holliday. I stayed in touch with Jeff Morey, Jack Burrows, and William Shillingberg through the dry spell and learned from them. When Casey Tefertiller began doing research for his biography of Earp, he contacted me, and I had to unpack my boxes, and I was soon hooked on the subject again. In the years since then, I think I have a clearer picture of him. Personally, Earp was a courageous, strong-willed, dour, quiet man, who commanded respect from quite a few good men. He also had a quick temper, which he generally controlled but occasionally broke loose, as in the case of his fight with Bill Smith in Wichita, Tom McLaury on the street in Tombstone, and during the Vendetta ride, although the last was tied to an ethos of taking the law into his own hands when the courts failed. He was a would-be entrepreneur who never quite made it but affiliated himself with conservative Republican businessmen as agent and friend. He made the mistake of living to old age and watching his reputation sullied, which caused him to seek vindication by telling his own story—which didn't turn out too well even though Lake made him into a legendary figure.

EW: Let's switch gears and talk about Doc Holliday. What sparked your interest in him?

GLR: First, I suppose it was the fact that he grew up forty miles from where I grew up, which gave me a connection to him, linked him to the same Southern heritage that I inherited, and somehow made him more human. Second, while Wyatt Earp is arguably the more important figure, Doc Holliday was more interesting to me—and apparently to generations dating literally back to the 1880s. Doc's arrest in Denver in 1882 introduced him to a broad newspaper audience, and during his Colorado years, he was the frequent subject of newspaper columns. Bat Masterson and Wyatt Earp left very different images of him, which he was a minor character in stories of Wyatt Earp in the first movies about (or, at least not the dapper, tragic figure he would become), but by the time of *Frontier Marshal* and *My Darling Clementine*, he competed with for audience attention with Earp. An early negative view of him portrayed Doc as an irascible, unlikeable sort (following the lead of Bat Masterson) In TV's *The Life and Legend of Wyatt Earp*, he was a supporting character who underscored Earp's nobility and honor with his sour personality and questionable character. I suspect that was because of the influence of Stuart Lake who clearly did not know what to do with Holliday, whom he appeared to view as a blemish on Earp's story. But, in movies from *Frontier Marshal* and *My Darling Clementine* through *The Gunfight at the O. K. Corral* to *Tombstone* and Kevin Costner's *Wyatt Earp* he challenged Earp as a character, in some instances clearly being the more complex and interesting. Earp seemed simple, if not good, whereas Doc was a more cynical figure, educated and tragic with a wry sense of humor.

EW: Many people know Doc Holliday as portrayed by Val Kilmer in 1993's *Tombstone*. Who was the real man and what were his motivations?

GLR: Kilmer is doubtless the most memorable Doc, although in some respects Dennis Quaid played Doc well. If only he had had better lines! The appeal of Doc is that he is a tragic figure. He was a cultured, educated man with a complement of Southern qualities that he used with skill at times. His interviews in Denver in 1882, while he was under arrest, are fascinating and reveal both his charm and his education. Family was extremely important to him, and I think that was a factor that drew him to the Earps, when he was distant from his own family. One thing is sure, though, he was not Wyatt's lap dog. They were together, off and on, for only four years. He was a bitter person and, at times, even self-pitying. He was embittered by his mother's death, by his father's quick remarriage to a much younger woman, and by the onset of consumption, and perhaps with a frustrated relationship with his first cousin, Mattie. When he left Georgia—on the run, I believe, rather than because of consumption—he was angry. He tried to pursue his career as a dentist, but he had been introduced into the world of saloons and gambling halls by a man named Lee Smith in Georgia (with whom he remained in contact through the years) and with all that weighed on him, he was drawn back into that world and the remedies for consumption common at the time—liquor and laudanum. I do not believe he had a death wish, as some claim. He was loyal to his friends (and he had more than some would have you believe), sometimes to his detriment, as in the case of Bill Leonard. He was without fear even as a child, and he nurtured that trait through the years. He stayed alive with a willingness to kill more than with a record of killing. He had a sardonic sense of humor and was a fair hand with a pen from the few examples of his writing that we have. He was generous and kind to children. He was hot-tempered at times, especially when drinking. His relationship with Kate was always troubled, but they shared a common loyalty to each other—or at least a dependency--that lasted until Tombstone. In his last years, he became well-known in the press and increasingly frail, which affected his ability to play cards and use a pistol. At that point, he was living mainly on his reputation—alone and, at times, virtually penniless, with only the letters of his sweet cousin Mattie, his contacts Lee Smith and Zan Griffith, and a few Leadville friends for comfort. Twice in his last year he worked guarding mining properties. He saw Wyatt and his father one last time each. If he had not met Wyatt Earp, he would have probably been just one more consumptive sport like so many others whose names are all but forgotten.

EW: As always, we close with a bit of mentorship. What advice do you want to pass along to the next generation of historians?

GLR: As the beneficiary of many historians, writers, and researchers, I know the importance of listening to and learning from others and for persistent review and research on my own conclusions. I would urge others to pursue the things that interest them—that is where the passion will be—rather than what others tell them they should do. Many people told me that Wyatt Earp and Doc Holliday had been overworked, and I listened to that advice on a few occasions. I learned from the efforts and like to think I made a few ancillary contributions in the process, but I was pulled back to my primary interests and led into related matters that informed my views and understanding, including forcing me to change my interpretations. So, here are a few pieces of advice (most of which I learned from others). First, if you're going to write about the "Wild West," throw a wide loop in your approach. Specifically, approach your subject in a broad context. That means reading and understanding things beyond your particular interest. The "Age of the Gunfighter" took place in the last forty years of the nineteenth century. Learn what was going on in the United States during that period, what forces were shaping American life, something about the organization and law of the territories and states where your subject occurred, something about the particular towns or regions that encompass your topic. Learn something about the social structure of American life. J. Frank Dobie told me in

1961 (the letter is on the wall next to my desk) that I needed a broad sense of history in order to write the particular history I wished to write. I've tried to follow his advice, and I think it has paid off. If you don't this you may think something is unique that isn't, you may misunderstand what events really meant, and you may be tempted to impose modern standards on the past that are inappropriate or just plain wrong. Second, working with a hypothesis is fine, but don't make your conclusions before you do your research. As one historian taught my generation, as a historian, we should not care what the truth is. We should only be concerned with finding it, whatever it is. Setting out to prove Wyatt Earp was a hero or a villain is not history's task; the task is to find out what sort of person he was. You do your research and draw your conclusions, not decide who he was and then find the evidence that will support your predetermined conclusion. Making a case is easier than finding the truth. Third, be willing to change your mind about things. I can review my writings and see how my view of many subjects I've studied has changed. On the other hand, some of my conclusions have stood up well against revision. Some years ago, I wrote an article on the street fight for *True West* called "The Fremont Street Fiasco" which argued that the O. K. Corral affair was not a victory of law over outlaw or the murder of innocent cowboys, but rather that it was a blunder, an unpremeditated series of miscalculations and misunderstandings that led to a fight that neither side really wanted. That's basically still my position because the research I've done since has tended to confirm it. Fourth, learn from those you disagree with. Ponder what they say. Consider their evidence. Look for both their errors and their points well-made. Familiarize yourself with the literature, not just what has been written in the past few years. You may find some insights that will help you. At the very least, you will be better informed. Dialogue—even if it is just reading different interpretations—may well surprise you, and you could find things that my generation and earlier generations missed. Fifth, don't assume that previous researchers have found everything. Newspapers are more accessible than they've ever been, and I can tell you for certain that researchers have found items from the Tombstone newspapers within the past couple of years that me and everybody else had missed who had gone through the papers—not to mention the fact that from time to time new copies of issues we didn't previously have available to us show up and reveal something previously undiscovered. And widen the loop on your sources. When Casey Tefertiller researched his biography of Earp, he read widely in California newspapers and found a bonanza of important material. I found material on Doc Holliday in Fort Griffin and other points in Texas in the Galveston newspapers. New things are still being found in newspapers east and west of Dodge City that have articles about the Earps. I found information on Tom Smith and the Bear River Riot in the Cincinnati, Ohio, newspapers. And the same is true of any topic, as Peter Brand and Kenneth Vail have proven. Finally, in summary, keep an open mind about your topic, question your conclusions, use your imagination in broadening your research, and find people you can trust to test some of your ideas on. It is a lot easier to correct something you write BEFORE it is published than afterwards. If the past twenty-five years have proven anything it is that there is still much to do in light of everything that has been found during those years. The field is alive, and it is so much richer once we get past simple good guys and bad guys.

Peter Brand of Sydney, New South Wales, Australia, is a legend in the realm of Western historians. A methodical researcher, Brand has authored several books including biographies of Perry Mallon and "Texas Jack" Vermillion and Doc Holliday nemesis Johnny Tyler. He is also the author of many popular and scholarly articles on Earp-era Tombstone and beyond. Brand is the world's foremost expert on the so-called Earp Vendetta Posse having fleshed out the details of the posse members in a series of lengthy papers which received high acclaim.

EW (Erik Wright): Let's talk about Ben Sippy. Your recent two-part paper on the mysterious Tombstone resident and career criminal gained much attention from readers of the *Journal*. What prompted you to begin looking into fleshing out Sippy's full story?

PB (Peter Brand): Ben Sippy had always been a curious character in the Tombstone story. Very little was known of him prior to Tombstone and absolutely nothing had been researched on him after he left. He beat Virgil Earp in the November 1880 election for the Tombstone City Marshal's job after the death of the incumbent, Fred White, in October. Virgil Earp had been living in Tombstone for one year at the time of the election, and he was already a deputy US marshal for Arizona Territory. His brother, Wyatt, had been a very efficient and successful deputy sheriff of Pima County and it seemed to me that Virgil should have won that election, given the Earps' prominence in the community at the time.

I became intrigued by the man who beat Virgil – Ben Sippy. I thought that if I could research his background and past experiences, I might be able to explain his ability to gain the necessary support to win the top lawman position in Tombstone. Further to that point, I wanted to learn what may have caused his sudden departure from Tombstone seven months later, while still holding the marshal's position.

What I found surprised me, but I think I was successful in that I exposed, for the first time, Sippy's very troubled upbringing and his long criminal history. Part one of the story explained what shaped Sippy as a man, and the experiences that forged his tough and fearless countenance, which, when combined with his large physical stature, afforded him a menacing presence that was useful when working as the Tombstone City Marshal. (later to be renamed the Tombstone Chief of Police)

Part two of the Sippy biography explains what became of him after he abruptly left Tombstone while still in office. I discovered his steady descent into further crime and violence. He truly became a fulltime professional criminal and was incarcerated in at least five different state penitentiaries. This was important to the overall story, as it makes his time as a Tombstone lawman even more astonishing.

I have always maintained that the more we know about all the characters in the complicated Tombstone story, the more we can begin to fully understand why certain things happened the way they did, and how these men and women contributed to the overall narrative.

As a biographer, I was anxious to thoroughly explore Sippy's time after Tombstone – something that no one had been able to do previously. I was extremely pleased with the results, and I hope that by bringing Sippy out of the shadows, I have more fully advanced our general understanding of the hard men who made Tombstone such a tough town. Discovering a verified prison mug shot of Ben Sippy was also very satisfying, as I think most WWHA members enjoy viewing authentic photos of the Tombstone characters.

EW: Now let me ask about the elephant in the room: how do you manage to do this level of research from Australia?

PB: When I first started doing research on the Tombstone saga, I quickly realized that it was not an easy task and was by no means straightforward. By traveling to the USA and attending different "wild west" gatherings, I began to learn about the complicated collection of researchers and authors who inhabited the field. Learning who to trust and with whom to align oneself was essential to the process. I worked closely with Jean Smith of Safford, Arizona, who taught me the art of genealogical research and I made life-long friendships and associations with Tombstone/Earp historians such as Lee Siva, Roger Jay, Jeff Morey, Casey Tefertiller, and Gary Roberts. These people educated me in the power of primary research. The obvious tyranny of distance was partially overcome by the internet and the digital collection of historical documents and newspapers now available online. Many major research facilities now offer paid research services and this, too, has made access to important information a little easier. Having said that, some facilities have closed their "online" doors to foreign researchers such as myself. The Utah State Library and Archive, for example, has blocked all foreign online access to their holdings via the internet. So, challenges still exist, and I am sure more hurdles will come into play from time to time. When this happens, I have reached out to trusted friends in the USA who are more than willing to assist. I have worked with WWHA members such as yourself [Erik

Wright], Jean Smith, Ron Woggon, and Mike Mihaljevich, who have all been incredibly generous to me.

EW: Tell us about yourself. How did an Aussie get so interested in American history?

PB: My father was a professional artist who was employed in the 1950s and 1960s to draw and paint for pulp action magazines. He specialized in Westerns and Detective Noir. I developed a love of both genres through his work, and as I grew up in the 1960s, watching American TV westerns and movies, I was attracted to the stories and the characters of the wild west. They dominated our screens in that period, and I then developed a desire to learn the real stories on which many of these programs were based. That lead to a further eagerness to travel to the actual locations where the real stories took place and having done so, my love affair with the American West was complete.

EW: You are well known for your work on the Earp Vendetta Posse. Do you believe your research into those men we previously did not know much about help to change the landscape of outlaw-lawman studies particularly as it pertains to the Earp field?

PB: I would say that question may be better answered definitely by the readers of my articles and books. I can only hope that I have contributed to a greater understanding of the Vendetta men and the Tombstone/Earp story by bringing more characters into the spotlight, rather than leaving them simply as bit-part players. As mentioned previously, it is my belief that knowing more about all the Tombstone men and women adds to our overall understanding of the topic. I think my discovery of photos of Dan Tipton, Jack Johnson (John

Blount) and the real Texas Jack Vermillion, along with other Earp friends and enemies, such as Crooked Mouth Green, Ben Maynard, Tom Corrigan, and Ben Sippy certainly helped readers, at least from a visual perspective. Publication of biographical articles on Dan Tipton, Jack Johnson and his brothers, Sherman McMaster and Vermillion have deepened my own understanding of how these men were well equipped to assist Wyatt when he needed them most. Added to that, my discovery that Sherman McMaster had been a Texas Ranger, whose company had held Curly Bill captive for at least five months in Ysleta, Texas in 1878, really added spice to McMaster's complicated association with both the cowboys and the Earps. I hope my discovery of how and when Curly Bill made his escape for the Texas Rangers added a new chapter to his mysterious story. The search is ongoing, but I would like to think these few examples have added depth and greater understanding to the story as a whole.

EW: One of the hallmarks of your published research is an absolute attention to every detail. When do you decide to stop the investigation and begin writing? What other methods do you adhere to in your research and writing processes?

PB: When to stop researching and start writing is an age-old dilemma that impacts every researcher who wants to write biographies or episodes from larger stories. I, like most, want to include as much information pertinent to the story as possible, but, in my case, it is not always achievable, as I am usually writing about characters who have never had their story told before, meaning information can be hard to come by. My general rule is to exhaustively gather as much as I can and look at the information in chronological order. I assess what I have and then ask myself if any missing information is absolutely vital to the story, or can the story still stand without it. If the story relies heavily on the missing information, I continue the hunt. If, however, I deem the story to have achieved its purpose, even with the gaps or with missing information, I will start to write and then publish. Examples are seen in my book about the real Texas Jack Vermillion. I wanted to categorically reveal the real man, John Oberland Vermillion, and set the record straight, despite large gaps in his life story. I achieved that purpose. The Ben Sippy article is another example – I searched high and low for his death details and burial place. I never found them, but I surely showed how he lived and, by doing so, I think I achieved my purpose.

EW: You are a notoriously private man. But what other interests and passions drive you?

PB: I have always been basically a shy guy, so that lends itself to privacy I guess – intentional or otherwise. Away from the Wild West, I have a great love of two very different sports, Cricket, and Rugby League. I played both at high school with moderate success on the Cricket field. I have recently been researching the life and violent death of a Rugby League player from the 1960s who played for the major team here in Sydney that I support, so that may turn into a biography. I also have a passion for poetry and music, especially live music performances. I was taught piano from an early age, but never pursued it. I have an appreciation for great singer/songwriters, in particular those who can weave their original poetic lyrics to create stories. My personal favorites are American country/rock troubadour, Steve Earle and Canadian folk legend, Gordon Lightfoot.

EW: How do you stay motivated in your writing endeavors?

PB: My motivation to discover new information about the Tombstone topic has never really waned over the years. But life can throw rocks at you from time to time that means you have to deal with other important issues as a priority when they arise. The year 2020 was one such time. Travel was restricted into and out of Australia and even between states. The worldwide pandemic put us all on notice and reminded us that we cannot predict what might come our way, and that our ability to go where our passion takes us can be restricted through no fault of our own.

I love the journey of discovery, so researching people and places is not a chore for me. I continue to search and hunt for information about the lives of the Vendetta men and the Tombstone topic as much as a I can. If I do hit a really lean time in terms of research results, I have taken a break from the Tombstone topic and refreshed by researching and writing about unrelated, yet intriguing, topics for *Wild West* Magazine. These articles included the life and death of Colorado frontier private detective, J. W. Hawkins, and then the CSI style wild west murder case that resulted in the hanging of George Black in Laramie, Wyoming. In this way, I continued to try to hone my writing and research skills, while viewing different aspects and characters of the era.

EW: You have made many research trips over the years to the United States. What was your first trip and what impressions did that trip leave on you?

PB: My first tour of the USA was in September 1991. It was a five-week holiday that started my love affair with the country and its people. I met life-long friends, Jean, and Chuck Smith in Tombstone on that trip. I was impressed by the grandeur of the scenery, the generosity of the people I met, the hospitality of strangers and the diversity of the country in general. I have been coming back, almost annually, ever since.

EW: Do you have a favorite place in America to visit? Anywhere you haven't been yet that you would like to see?

PB: I must say that Arizona is still my favorite place to visit in America. The desert has a beauty of its own that reminds me in some ways of outback Australia. But, unlike Australia, Arizona also has much higher elevations where you have alpine scenery and seasonal snow. Its history, scenery and people keep me coming back.

There are several places I have not yet visited, but I want to see Alaska. It seems like the last frontier and its pristine beauty put it at the top of my list.

EW: What historians did you admire when you first began and why? What message or advice would you like to pass on to future historians?

PB: When I first started to explore the Tombstone topic I was drawn to several authors and historians who demonstrated a conviction to the facts of the story, rather than the legend. Those people included Casey Tefertiller, Gary Roberts, and Jeff Morey. Many other writers seemed unable to separate the legend from the fact. Some filled in gaps with falsehoods, or merged fact with fiction to the point where it was impossible for the reader to distinguish between the two.

I decided that the truth was far more important to me than the legend, or fiction, and I decided to search for primary sources when writing, and only use secondary sources from reliable authors who followed the same path.

The advice that I would give to future historians and researchers is to look for primary sources and to dig deep when searching records. Persistence and patience are the keys to finding new information. Do not give up the hunt, because learning more about our history is a meaningful and very satisfying pursuit.

Richard W. Etulain, a deeply respected historian of the American West, Etulain has written and edited over sixty publications over his career. Among his many books are critical assessments of frontier culture, literature, and art as well as biographies of Billy the Kid, Calamity Jane, Abraham Lincoln, and others. He is past president of both the Western Literature Association and the Western History Association.

EW (Erik Wright): Your new book *Abraham Lincoln: A Western Legacy* shifts focus on a man who is largely remembered as an "eastern" president while others, like Teddy Roosevelt, are remembered as "western" presidents. Describe this book and your desire to shed more light on Lincoln's western contributions.

RWE (Richard W. Etulain): My first interests in Abraham Lincoln and the American West resulted from boyhood experiences and later academic training. A grade schoolteacher led me to an interest in and admiration for Lincoln, a draw that continued and expanded throughout high school and college. I bought Lincoln books and wrote about him when I got an opportunity. Then, off to graduate school and a doctorate with a specialty in the American West.

Later, a history professor colleague, knowing of my fascination with Lincoln and my training in western subjects, encouraged me to think about Lincoln and the West. Bingo.

I began to look at the ways Lincoln connected with the West. He thought of himself (in Illinois) as a Man of the West, but gradually he became involved in western subjects and people: taking a stance against the possible expansion of slavery beyond the Mississippi, and supporting railroads, famers and farming, and friends who were living in the West.

As president (1861-65), even during the heavy, heavy pressures of the Civil War and executive leadership, Lincoln kept up with western topics: the possible expansion of slavery, Indian conflicts, territorial needs, railroads, farming, and land management. As I looked at Lincoln's presidency, it amazed me to see his ongoing interests in the West in the midst of leading a country divided by a horrendous war. I set out to examine and point out Lincoln's links to the West, to cast light on a subject not many previous writers had emphasized.

EW: How did Lincoln contribute to the construction of America's first transcontinental railroad?

RWE: Lincoln entered the White House primarily with Whig political backgrounds, a political party he followed for nearly 20 years from the early 1830s until the early 1850s. The Whigs, who had begun as a party opposing what they considered Andrew Jackson's over-the-top presidential domination, wanted Congress to legislate and the president to administer. This Whiggish philosophy influenced Lincoln's moves as president concerning the railroads.

Lincoln had a long, strong history with railroads. He pushed for their establishment in Illinois and served as a leading lawyer for the Illinois Central Railroad. He argued in support of the railroads in important court cases.

So, Lincoln favored railroads and their expansion when he entered the White House. He made clear to members of Congress that he would support a transcontinental railroad when the legislative branch began discussion of that possibility in 1861-62. Once Congress actually launched its deliberations on the legislation, Lincoln backed the idea and behind the scenes encouraged the legislation. In July 1862, Lincoln happily signed the Pacific Railroad Act planning a railroad route to the West Coast.

EW: What is Lincoln's legacy in the West?

RWE: Although I have tried in three books and many other writers have attempted in their books and essays to show Lincoln's shaping influences on the West, not many general readers think of Lincoln as a major figure in western history. That's not surprising considering how much Americans are locked into the Civil War as a terrible conflict between the North and the South.

Unfortunately, those tied to the North-South framework fail to see Lincoln's large influences on the West. Those influences were (1) opposition to the spread of slavery into the trans-Mississippi West; (2) support for the launching of the transcontinental railroads; (3) backing for the Homestead Act providing lands for families and soldiers moving west; (4) encouragement of the Morrill Land Act founding land-grant educational institutions; (5) and attention to the establishing or administrating of numerous western territories.

Finally, as our greatest president, Lincoln also shaped the West, as he did the rest of the country, with his superb leadership, moral stances, and balanced decisions.

EW: Over the span of your career, you have authored dozens of books ranging from topics like Wallace Stegner, Calamity Jane, César Chávez, and Billy the Kid. What draws you to these subjects?

RWE: I'm in love with the history and literature of the West; in fact, some think I am fanatical about the West. At first, I was drawn to literary history because I had college degrees in both English and history. So, I was attracted early on to Stegner and his writings because he was an outstanding example of a first-rate western novelist and historian. Undoubtedly, I was drawn, in part, to César Chávez because of my Spanish-Basque backgrounds, and also because of my interest in farm and ranch workers.

Toward the end of my teaching career, I looked around for the life story of a leading demigod - e.g., Custer, Hickok, Earp, Billy the Kid, or an Indian leader - that needed to be told to general audiences. I discovered that all these figures had several biographies - but not Calamity

Jane. So, I spent several years researching her complicated life. Finally, I lived and taught twenty-two years in New Mexico and was often drawn to Billy the Kid as the most-written-about New Mexican. Onward to Señor Billy in two books.

Nor should I skip over my lifetime interest in biography. From Abraham Lincoln to the western heroes/heroines and on to other figures like Oregon governor and senator Mark Hatfield, and finally to my own early years in a ranch memoir, I have been intrigued with the unfolding lives of numerous peoples. Fads in historical writing come and go, but biography endures. I discovered that in my long research and writing career.

EW: In your book *Stegner: Conversations on History and Literature* (1983) you present a series of discussions with noted novelist, historian, and conservationist Wallace Stegner. Along with the late Edward Abbey, Stegner is remembered as one of the greatest writers of the American west. Describe Stegner and his views on driving the historical narrative. Was he an optimist for the west or did he see it as a dying landscape?

RWE: It is misleading to think of Wallace Stegner's attitudes about the West in either-or terms; instead, we should think of him in both-and terms. For example, he could salute the conservation efforts of John Wesley Powell and other like-minded westerners. He also spoke of wilderness as "the geography of hope" in his most important environmental statement. But he could be quite critical of large corporations who were misusing natural resources to line their pockets or of individuals abusing western lands.

Even more important than settings and landscapes to Stegner were the actions of humans. For example, in three of his most important novels - *The Big Rock Candy Mountain* (1943), *Angle of Repose* (1971), *Crossing to Safety* (1987) - his heroes and heroines are those who struggle through individual jungles and deserts of challenges and decisions and yet retain their moral standards, balance, and fairness. Stegner was primarily an optimist about present-day society and the future - if Americans were fair-minded, committed to others, and willing to accept their own limitations. Environmental miscues and harmful human actions did not drive him into the camp of the pessimists.

EW: What shaped your upbringing as a historian and writer?

RWE: The first, molding influences were my mother and grandmother. They bought me books and took me to the town library. Even before my teens, I was a bibliomaniac. Then, as a college student, I dreamed of writing. As a graduate student, I knew as an ambitious professor I had to write for publication.

Along the way, I became enamored with the fiction and histories of Wallace Stegner and aspired to try one of his middle-of-the-road ventures, literary history. It struck home.

More than anything I have been a literary historian, writing about Stegner, Ernest Haycox, historical novels generally, and fiction dealing with such figures as Calamity Jane, Billy the Kid, Mary Lincoln, and the Southwest and the Northwest.

I also moved ahead with writing overview histories of the American West, first with fellow historian Michael Malone, and then on my own. Along the way, I've also produced books on western historical writing, western films, and religious topics.

EW: Talk about your assessment of Billy the Kid. How much of the myth surrounding outlaws like the Kid have plagued the research process?

RWE: Researching and writing about Billy the Kid allowed me to put to work the complexities I had discovered in my career of writing. Over time, I realized I could neither entirely condemn Billy as a murdering rascal or wholly praise him as an adventurous young man to travel with. Instead, I had to take both - and approach, seeing his negative as well as his positive sides. The mythmakers of Billy had seen both sides of Billy, as a rogue and as warm companion; but not at the same time. For me, coming closest to understanding a controversial figure like the Kid was to see and picture him as a complex human, with conflicting tendencies.

Often, historians, biographers, and other writers shy away from writing both-and complex life stories because they see such accounts as waffling, as not moving either one way or another. For me, I have increasingly concluded that these middling, complex stories of the Wild West characters, or even of such figures as presidents George Washington, Abraham Lincoln, and Bill Clinton and Jimmy Carter are nearer to the complicated truth than accounts swinging decisively to one side or the other.

EW: What advice do you wish to leave with the next generation of western historians?

RWE: There are a few bits of advice I hope will strike fallow ground with historians to come. First, realize the varying draws and viewpoints that characterize writings about the American West. Some authors, mainly lay or general historians, love the dramatic and romantic Old West, the West of the nineteenth century, illustrated in dime novels, John Wayne films, and Zane Grey and Louis L'Amour Westerns. On the other hand, academic historians in recent times have been more interested in racial and ethnic, gender, and environmental themes. All of us should recognize these two pathways, accept them, and work vigorously in our preferred path of the two, emphasizing the strengths of our approach and avoiding throwing critical darts at opposing views.

Second, I encourage those in love with the West to read widely and not make snap decisions about the "truth" of the West. We learn new things in changing times, we uncover new bits of history, and we should be willing to change our attitudes and conclusions. As examples, we think different about the roles of Indians in western history than in the period up to the 1960s. Our views of women's participation in western history have sharply shifted since the 1960s.

Finally, travel your own path. Find out what works for you and move ahead. Through the years, I have repeatedly heard the words of my father's heavily accented English (he was an immigrant Spanish Basque sheepherder and rancher): "getter done." Those words have helped push me through my output of 60 books, authored or edited. I encourage others to grab the subjects that mean most to you and find your niche to write about those topics. Onward…

Jerome A. Greene is a celebrated author and historian who has written extensively on the Plains Indian Wars of the frontier west. In *Nez Perce Summer, 1877*, Greene deftly gives the account of this campaign which stretched from Idaho, Wyoming, and Montana territories, but lasted just under four violent months.

EW (Erik Wright): General William Tecumseh Sherman said that the Nez Perce War in 1877 was "one of the most extraordinary Indian wars of which there is any record." What sets this conflict apart from the others?

JAG (Jerome A. Greene): Sherman here focused on several peculiarities--one being that these Indians refrained from the practice of scalping. They further allowed captive women to go free. Nor did they attack and kill peaceful families. Also, as Alvin M. Josephy, Jr., explained in his foreword to my book, they "fought with almost scientific skill, using advance and rear guards, skirmish lines, and field fortifications." Their homeland occupied part of present northeastern Washington State but included lands in today's northeastern Oregon in the Snake and Salmon rivers.

EW: Who are the Nez Perce people and what role did they play in the conquest of the West?

JAG: The Nez Perce (French, and formally pronounced *Nay Pairsay*) composed a small tribe occupying part of present northeastern Washington, as well as lands in today's northeastern Oregon. Like other native tribes in the West, their homeland was beset by the intrusion of whites seeking land and other resources in their country. The Nez Perce--like other tribes before them--faced the uncertainties imposed by the presence of whites among them that ultimately threatened the people and their homeland.

EW: Set the scene: what was happening in the West in 1877 that sparked the Nez Perce War?

JAG: By 1877 much of the land in the West had been (or was being) similarly occupied by whites moving onto what they supposed was free land. Most sought land for farming and cattle raising, while many others responded to newly discovered riches promised by latent gold and silver. That was the broad impetus that drew to the West many from the East, thereby promoting the intrusions on native lands.

EW: Why is this conflict not as well remembered as other engagements such as the Custer Campaign or the Apache Wars?

JAG: Simply put, the Nez Perces involved a smaller tribe of people, whereas the various Apache wars and Sioux and Cheyenne campaigns dealt with much larger bodies of native people often covering larger acreage to include a variety of tribes--some in more or less formal alliances, too--compared with the smaller body of Nez Perces. Moreover, Custer had been a prominent military leader during the Civil War and was already therefore well known.

EW: You have written extensively on the history of the Indian Wars. Talk about your professional background and how you first became interested in the subject.

JAG: My interest in Indian people goes back to my youth, when I participated in in YMCA and Boy Scout activities dealing with Native American themes, including Indian dancing. I grew up in northern New York State, and as a kid hunted relics along the shores of Lake Ontario and the St. Lawrence River. In junior high school I read books on Custer and Buffalo Bill Cody, etc., and following my army service (in Oklahoma and Libya) I attended college and graduate school in South Dakota and Oklahoma. I worked three seasons as a park ranger at the then Custer Battlefield--now Little Bighorn Battlefield National Monument, -- and taught two years at what is now Haskell Indian Nations University in Kansas. (My first book was *Evidence and the Custer Enigma*--and was based largely on my work at the then-Custer Battlefield.) I've written twenty-four books as well as many articles on these subjects while in graduate school and since, and I've further taught many courses on these subjects.

EW: What are some common myths and misconceptions when it comes to the Indian Wars?

JAG: There are many myths about the Indian wars in the trans-Mississippi West. Perhaps the most common is that they were seemingly over in a heartbeat, when actually the warfare, however sporadic it appeared, carried on for better than forty years, say, from the 1850s until 1900, with even a few brief episodes after that. Another is that Custer was a general when he was killed at the Little Bighorn. Custer served as a brigadier and a major general during the Civil War; following the war, when the army was reorganized, he served as a lieutenant colonel, although he held a brevet (or honorary) rank as a major general (and was entitled to be *called* "general") although his pay and station was that held by a lieutenant colonel. He never would serve as a general officer again. Another myth was that his hair was long and flowing as in the famous "Last Stand" pictures. It was cut short--very short--before the troops left Fort Lincoln, Dakota Territory.

Another might be that the soldiers used lever-action repeating rifles and carbines, when in reality they used breech-loading single shot rifles (infantry) and carbines (cavalry).

EW: You co-wrote a book on the Sand Creek Massacre in 2013. Discuss the importance of that massacre and the site's importance to the Cheyenne and Arapaho peoples.

JAG: Sand Creek proved a devastating blow to the Southern Cheyennes and Arapahos and ended--for a time--their domination on the southern plains. The troops under Colonel John M. Chivington essentially committed a slaughter of those people, and the event remains one of the most disturbing events in all American history. Under congressional direction, in 1998, the National Park Service--along with participation of Southern Cheyenne and Arapaho descendants--through research and ground-truthing, and the help of volunteers and local landowners, at long last verified the site of the massacre in eastern Colorado, producing a wealth of evidence in the process. In so doing, the study team in its site determination in fact validated the memories of the Cheyennes and Arapahos, who have since sanctioned the location where the massacre occurred based on the historical and archeological findings.

EW: The field recently lost Robert "Bob" Utley. In his memoir *Custer and Me: A Historian's Memoir,* Utley mentions you several times. What influence did Utley have on your career and what legacy does he leave in his wake?

JAG: Bob Utley was *the* major impetus for my National Park Service career. Like him, I served as a ranger-historian at the then-Custer Battlefield National Monument in Montana--but in 1968, 1970, and 1971--some thirty years after Bob. I met him there in '68 and again in 1970. He offered me a job in Washington, D.C., as a Research Historian, but I'd already taken a teaching job at Haskell College in Kansas teaching American Indian history. When that job terminated in 1971, Bob facilitated my joining the National Park Service as a research historian at the newly established Denver Service Center for the purposes of the National Park Service Bicentennial program. Bob was a meticulous researcher and writer significant in his ability to project knowledge of Native Americans with clarity and respect. His books always reflected solid analysis and ever-meaningful prose, and he venerated Native American views. His contributions always reflected solid analysis and ever-meaningful prose. He was a very dear friend.

Michael Hiltzik is a Pulitzer Prize-winning journalist and author having written extensively for the Los Angeles Times and other publications. He is the author of several books including *Iron Empires: Robber Barons, Railroads, and the Making of Modern America*.

EW (Erik Wright): What did the completion of the transcontinental railroad mean for America and the theory of manifest destiny?

MH (Michael Hiltzik): The transcontinental railroad was both an expression of Manifest Destiny and its driver forward. The railroad began as a symbol of America's determination to extend its reach coast to coast and provided the means to do so. The railroad's penetration into the western prairie, for instance, was seen by American business and political leaders as a tool for herding Native American tribes together and moving them out of the way of "civilization"—that is, white civilization. Railroads built with government help were granted large swaths of vacant territory on terms that encouraged them to import settlers from the East and from Europe.

EW: Who were the robber barons and what role did they play in the development of American railroad infrastructure?

MH: These tycoons were the first business celebrities in American history. As James Bryce, a Scottish diplomat who wrote sort of a sequel to Tocqueville's *Democracy in America* in 1888, observed, "The railway kings are among the greatest men, perhaps I may say are the greatest men, in America…. They have fame, for everyone has heard of their achievements; every newspaper chronicles their movements. They have power, more power—that is, more opportunity of making their personal will prevail—than perhaps anyone in political life."

Some "robber barons," such as J. P. Morgan, E.H. Harriman, and Cornelius Vanderbilt, played a positive role in the railroads' development by mustering capital and imposing novel, and modern, management methods on the fragmented and fractious industry.

But they and others also undermined the buildout of the industry by manipulating railroad securities, saddling their lines with debt, and competing with each other in wasteful ways. Some of the earliest tycoons were more interested in trading railroad securities for their own profits than building and maintaining the physical infrastructure. This left many lines financially crippled. Securities of one line, the Erie, was so assiduously bought and sold for the profits of manipulators that it became known as "the scarlet woman of Wall Street."

EW: The Gilded Age was a defining chapter in the history of America. What was life like for Americans during this period and what was the outlook for America as it moved towards the 20th century?

MH: The original Gilded Age bears amazing similarities to the period we have been living through. It was a time of ostentatious wealth, widely reported in the popular press for the appetite of its readers for news of the rich and newly famous.

But we also started to see rising economic inequality, especially during the slumps that recurred throughout the late 19th century. Layoffs swept through the railroad industry, idling workers who had no resources for survival. As a result, we saw the founding of the first nationwide labor union, the Knights of Labor, and the first significant broad strike: The Pullman strike of 1894 began as a protest of mass layoffs of workers at Pullman's plant in Chicago, while he refused to reduce rents at his company town. The strike spread across the Midwest until it was put down by the federal government.

EW: Describe the research and writing process that went into Iron Empires. Did you face any memorable challenges?

MH: I researched the book in archives and libraries in New York, California, St. Paul and elsewhere, as well as contemporary memoirs, newspapers, and financial records and journals. At the Morgan Library in New York, I consulted the handwritten journals of Fanny Morgan, Pierpont Morgan's wife, to tell the story of the Morgans' cross-country trip on the transcontinental railroad just weeks after its completion.

For the cultural aspects of the story, I relied on "The Gilded Age," the 1873 satire by Mark Twain and Charles Dudley Warner that gave the period its name; I also quote extensively from the poetry and prose of Walt Whitman, which reflect the waxing and waning of American esteem for the railroads and their owners.

Some of the challenges arose because American businesses have left their historical archives to deteriorate. The Union Pacific Railroad, for instance, now has only a single librarian overseeing its archives of its 150-year history; she was unable to retrieve any of the materials I sought about the railroad because she has no staff. Another challenge was that E.H. Harriman did not keep a journal himself or write his memoirs; for his story I relied on the detailed recollections of his associates and the record of his groundbreaking expedition to Alaska in 1898, which is at the Smithsonian.

EW: How did the major railroad companies manage labor relations with their workers as they feverishly worked to lay track across the landscape?

MH: At first, the free market worked. There was so much demand for skilled and unskilled workers as the railroads competed with each other to lay track that wages soared (at least, in 19th century terms). The railroads stationed recruiters at Eastern docks to snare emigrants as they got off the boats from Europe, offering them high wages, housing, and guaranteed work even after the first wave of construction ended—that in the hopes that they would stay out west and help develop the territory the railroads served.

But when economic downturns came, the workers were the first casualties. Their wages were slashed, and layoffs swept across the industry, fomenting the labor unrest described above. "Boomers"—the skilled workers accustomed to moving from railroad to railroad offering their services—expected to have landed in a permanent growth industry, but they were wrong. The railroads, facing high fixed financing costs, thought they had no choice but to find cost cuts on the labor side.

As layoffs continued, the same railroad tycoons who had basked in the admiration of the public soon found themselves condemned as, yes, robber barons.

EW: After the completion of the transcontinental railroad was completed did interest in the railroads begin to wane?

MH: The first transcontinental railroad was followed by the construction of more. By the turn of the century, there were five competing lines. The quest to secure entry into Chicago, the hub of the national system, is what eventually set Morgan and Harriman at each others' throats and caused the tumultuous battle at the climax of "Iron Empires."

EW: What is the legacy of these workers and companies today?

MH: America's railroads have been overtaken as freight shippers by trucking and air. But their legacy still remains, physically crisscrossing the continent and in financial terms through the modern management techniques that they pioneered. They were America's first big business, and their history can still be read from coast to coast.

Charles Rankin spent years as the associate director and editor-in-chief for the University of Oklahoma Press, one of the leading publishers for non-fiction frontier history. Prior to his tenure in Oklahoma, Rankin was the director of publications for the Montana Historical Society Press and editor of *Montana: The Magazine of Western History*.

EW (Erik Wright): You recently guest-edited a special issue of *South Dakota History* which features previously unpublished work on Wild Bill Hickok by the late historian James D. McLaird. How did you get involved in that project?

CR (Charles Rankin): Jim McLaird was an author of mine when I was Editor-in-Chief at the University of Oklahoma Press. (I am retired now.) After Jim completed his definitive biography, *Calamity Jane: The Woman and the Legend*, and we published it in 2005, I contracted him to write a biography of Wild Bill Hickok. Jim was a slow but sure worker, and several years passed. He and I stayed in touch, but, surprising to us all, Jim passed away unexpectedly in August 2017. He had completed some nine chapters of his Hickok biography, but when his widow Donna McLaird sent them to me, it was obvious they were not ready for publication. But some of the material was, although not as a book, if someone would work on it. When OU Press agreed to cancel the contract, Nancy Koupal, Director of Publications at the South Dakota State Historical Society, and I discussed taking those parts of the manuscript that held promise, weaving them together, confirming sources, and polishing them up for journal publication. The result was the special guest-edited issue on Wild Bill.

EW: Many people may remember McLaird from his work on Calamity Jane and his groundbreaking biography of Hugh Glass. Unfortunately, McLaird passed away in 2017. Can you talk about what kind of a man and historian McLaird was?

CR: As Nancy Koupal told me more than once, Jim McLaird, then a professor of history at Dakota Wesleyan University, was her most dependable go-to historian for advice on South Dakota history. That had always been my experience at OU Press as well. Jim was almost frustratingly fair, so balanced and accommodating were his critiques of other people's work. Loved by his students, he was a quiet gentleman who loved South Dakota history and was long fascinated with sorting facts from legend as they related to some of the most celebrated Old West characters we know. He was especially interested in Calamity Jane and Wild Bill Hickok because of their South Dakota connections.

EW: Hickok represents the archetypal gunfighter. What drew McLaird to explore his story? Did he make any new discoveries concerning Hickok's life?

CR: Jim McLaird's approach was historical in the sense that he would start with the most solid historical information he could find (and he left no stone unturned), and then trace the evolution, repetition, and morphing of that information into myths and legends. Like any historian or writer worth his or her salt, Jim depended heavily on Joe Rosa, who discovered more new factual information about Hickok than any other single researcher. Jim's contribution was to show how myth and legend had grown up despite that information to shape, color, and obscure what we know or think we know about Hickok.

Just one example: as Jim shows in his *South Dakota History* articles, James Butler Hickok supposedly died holding a poker hand of aces and eights, yet no one at the time of Hickok's death in 1876 or subsequently noted that fact until a latter-day biographer "revealed" it fifty years later (in 1926). In fact, Jim provides evidence that Hickok had just folded a hand when he was shot in that Deadwood saloon and that very likely, no new hand had even been dealt. Still, aces and eights are too much fun to not believe. Jim understood that, too. It's one of those legends that, if it isn't true, it ought to be. Jim just wanted us to understand it for what it is: folklore.

EW: You have served as the editor-in-chief for the University of Oklahoma Press for many years. Talk about your passion for the American West and how scholarly works on the West have evolved over time.

CR: Like it or not, the American West is the place of romance, and not just in the nineteenth century. Twentieth-century western history may be more environmentally oriented, but there are still plenty of heroes and gawd-awful villains to write about, not to mention issues and events that not only surprise and fascinate but are relevant. Well-researched, well-written non-fiction on the American West used to have a secure home among a handful of university presses and state historical societies. Except for the South Dakota Historical Society Press, that's not very true anymore. But western non-fiction still fascinates and still draws the attention of the publishing world, often from for-profit publishers, whether among the big publishing houses in New York City or among the smaller independents out West. Some of that work is very, very good, and some of it is not good at all. But that's nothing new. Non-fiction history is always only as good as the questions you ask of your material. Then, you have to have something to say, you have to say it well, and you have to construct a compelling story.

EW: What challenges do you foresee in regard to the field of Western history and its commercial appeal as we move deeper into the 21st-century?

CR: Relevance and getting your work recognized. Relevance because so much has been published about the household names and events of the Old West that often what gets published today is drivel or rehash. What is truly new can be said about George Armstrong Custer? Well, quite a bit, apparently, if you ask the right questions about your material, as T. J. Stiles did with his Pulitzer Prize-winning *Custer's Trials*. Relevance also relates to bringing great western history into the 20th and 21st centuries, and that's happening, I'm glad to say.

How to get your work recognized is the theme year-in and year-out with organizations like the Western Writers of America. There is so much competition and diversion from various forms of media today, and the attention span of even the reading public seems to be diminishing. But as a friend of mine once said also, you can't hold a good book down, not a *really* good book.

EW: The University of Oklahoma Press is one of just a few publishers left who continually publish and promote our frontier history. What obstacles do you face as an editor as many new historians seem to favor esoteric bits of history as opposed to the broad and popular images the world is familiar with?

CR: Esoteric bits of history are easy to focus on because they are small and manageable, and such studies can add to what we know in helpful ways. But they don't change the way we see things more broadly. Big-view history is hard, and it's even more difficult if you offer it in a way that affords a new perspective on what we think we know. That new perspective can't be whacky; it has to make sense. But if it expands the horizon of our views a little farther, helps us make a little more sense of the present by better understanding the past, then we have a book worth reading.

EW: As an editor you have worked alongside some of the most prestigious and well-respected historians in the field. What lessons have you learned in your role as editor-in-chief and what lessons do you hope to pass along to the next generation?

CR: Story. Because story is how we understand deeper truths. Believe it or not, I've been criticized by academic peers in the business for loving stories, for wanting to publish books that people want to read. Guilty as charged. What so many authors, especially academics but others, too, seem to forget is their audience. Sometimes they don't care; they freely admit their audience is the 5 or 10 other interested academics. But as Wallace Stegner said, if you want to make a difference, you have to catch the ear of the world. So, you have to ask: who are you writing for? It's not enough to ask yourself what authors you most admire. You have to ask what you admire about their writing. Facility with words and images is a must, yes, but in the end, it's going to be the power of the story that makes an author's work memorable.

David D. de Haas recently retired from a long career as an emergency room physician in the Los Angeles area. But beyond his medical knowledge he has an encyclopedic memory of the history of Earp-era Tombstone and has written several articles as well as his book, *The Earps Invade Southern California: Bootlegging Los Angeles, Santa Monica, and the Old Soldiers' Home.*

EW (Erik Wright): David, you recently retired from a career as an emergency room physician. Tell us about that life and what you are doing now in retirement.

DDH (David D. de Haas): Wow; retirement is so amazing! I just wish I had done it much earlier and most-definitely could have. I read all of the retirement literature in the years preceding my own, and something in one article really hit home for me and finally got me to call it quits. Obviously, the big worry we all have, which keeps us going/working, is we will retire too soon and possibly run out of money before we die; that would be devastating. This piece posed the question - What is even worse than retiring too early and running out of money before you die? Answer - waiting too long, and retiring too late, thereby missing out on a year or two of your deserved hard-earned retirement years, something you worked towards your whole life, and didn't take when you could have! More time with your friends and family you should have had and missed out on! It really got me thinking, lit a fire under me, and pushed me to finally pull the trigger, and take that plunge into retirement. That and on the frontline (and I mean ON THE FRONTLINE) dealing with the COVID-19 pandemic for two years, in addition to all the other bureaucratic nonsense that emergency physicians have to deal with daily. Emergency medicine is an extremely stressful job, definitely one of the most demanding out there. ER physicians make life and death decisions several times an hour every single shift. One mistake and someone could die, be maimed for life, or suffer unnecessary pain. In the later stages of your career, it becomes easier and easier to overthink all that and develop unnecessary anxiety.

    I've established such a wonderful daily routine since I retired, and absolutely love my new life I worked 40+ years to achieve. Although maintaining my medical license and keeping up to date on medical literature, I have never once thought of going back in the last 2+ years and never once been bored since I left practice. I sleep in every morning now until about 9 AM and then have a small breakfast while catching up with the latest news and evaluating the current day in the stock market. I then trade stocks for an hour or so and move my retirement savings around a bit to optimize my portfolio and stay current, and next switch over to my Wild West reading, research, and writing. After a few hours, I meet up with a group of my friends at the gym every afternoon and we all work out together for several hours. When I get home I have a late lunch, take a nap while watching TV, and then play with my grandchildren. Two of them live with us. After dinner, I spend a little more time with the grandkids playing in the backyard and watching the sunset over the Pacific Ocean, do a little more writing, and then Mary and I meet up, once the grandkids have gone to sleep, and watch a movie together nightly before bedtime. It's so fulfilling to catch up on all the hundreds of classic movies and TV shows I missed through the years while I was studying to become a doctor and then starting our young family. That's my typical day, and I love it! On the weekends, Mary and I spend more time together, playing in the backyard with our grandkids and going on long walks at the Dana Point Harbor, San Clemente Pier, or the historic downtown San Juan Capistrano area and Mission, all of which are close to our home, and then out for brunch.

EW: You have long been a vocal champion of the promotion and preservation of Wild West history. What first got you interested in the field?

DDH: As a young child, watching all the western TV shows that were airing every night. That's pretty much all there was in those days (the 1960s). Gunsmoke, Bonanza, The Rifleman, Wyatt Earp, Bat Masterson, Maverick, Wanted Dead or Alive, Have Gun Will Travel, Davy Crockett, and Zorro. The heroism/bravery, adventure, excitement, and romance of the Old West.

EW: Is there a particular era or personality from the frontier whom you find the most interesting? If so, why?

DDH: In my early childhood it was Davy Crockett from the Disney TV series. I progressed to Wyatt Earp, Doc Holliday, Bat Masterson, Billy the Kid, Pat Garrett, Tom Horn, Mickey Free, Albert Fountain (and his nemesis, the devious Albert Fall), and some of the range wars from there – Johnson County War and the Graham-Tewksbury feud (Pleasant Valley War).

EW: Tell us about your recent book *The Earps Invade Southern California*.

DDH: *The Earps Invade Southern California* is the never before told story of the Earps in Southern California in the Sawtelle (next to UCLA) and Santa Monica areas near the Old Soldiers' Home in the first decade of the 20th century. The Earps are the thread which ties this story together, but it's also a tale of bootlegging, speakeasies, early prohibition (before "Prohibition "), the development of Santa Monica, Los Angeles, Malibu, and the Hollywood areas, and how the Veterans Administration (V.A.) came about. The Earp brothers and their friends spent much more time together in this area than they did in any of the old cowtowns and mining camps that they are much more famous for, and it turns out to be a fascinating story.

EW: Did you uncover any surprising details about the Earps or their associates during your research for that book?

DDH: It's mind blowing how many of the Earps Tombstone friends lived and died in the Southern California area at the end of their careers. After the book came out, Don and I coauthored a featured article for *Wild West* magazine (October 2021) titled "The Earp's Fellow Sophisticates "which concentrated on this association a bit more. One especially interesting fact is that future 1881 OK Corral Gunfight Earp defense attorney, Thomas Fitch, had been the featured speaker six years earlier (in 1875) at the launching ceremony for the new ocean resort town of Santa Monica, California (just west of Sawtelle), and many former Tombstoners became intimately involved with that desirable area.

EW: How did that book add to the overall story of the Earp legend?

DDH: It goes into some detail about that previously "lost decade" in the lives of the Earp family, which isn't covered anywhere else. After all their years wandering about the Wild West, and before finally settling down, the Earp family was involved in a West Los Angeles bootlegging scheme in ~1901 - 1909.

EW: This leads to another interesting question: talk about your longtime collaborative partnership with historian Don Chaput. How did that begin and what kind of mentor has he been?

DDH: Don has been an amazing friend and mentor for me, and I'm so grateful he came into my life. I feel we are absolutely perfect partners for one another in that we each have skills, talents, and passions, the other lacks, while both having a mutual love for the Wild West but with divergent points of view, and together we complement one another perfectly. It's a synergistic relationship. We have now worked together on many projects and are currently collaborating on quite a few more you will be hearing about very soon.

We first met when we were both mutual best friends with author Lee Silva. I had already been close/best friends with Lee for a number of years before I finally I got up the nerve to ask him to introduce me to Don. Lee and Don had already known one another much longer, about 40 years. I had read all of Don's books and long admired his work; he was a big celebrity to me. Too intimidated to try approach him on my own, during one of our phone calls, I ended by timidly asking Lee if he would "one day" introduce me to Don. About a half hour after we hung up Lee unexpectedly called back and told me he had called

Don after our phone conversation and told him I wanted to meet him. He said that Don had heard of me and wanted to meet me too and that I should give him a call. I was devastated and very embarrassed, feeling like the guy who had told his close friend in confidence he liked a girl, and then having this trusted friend go and tell her behind his back. I had hoped Lee would do it much more slowly and subtly. I also couldn't believe that Don would actually be interested in meeting me. Thinking instead Lee was just trying to pacify me when he realized I was upset with him calling Don so soon, I didn't call Don out of humiliation. Well, a couple days passed, and Lee called me again, expressing that Don Chaput had called him on his own and was wondering why I had not yet called. Wow, I abruptly realized Don actually did want to speak with/meet me. I immediately called him, and we had a long phone conversation which ended up with an invitation to his home for dinner for my wife Mary and me, and together with his wife Toni. Well, we all got along fabulously, a wonderful evening together as if we had known each other for years and ended with Don offering to help me research a western magazine article I was working on and signing all his books for me (Don's is a very difficult/desired autograph to get) while giving me a few others I had not known about. "The rest is history!" I think Don and Toni saw me as a younger guy who could possibly carry on with some of the projects that he had not yet completed, and Toni even mentioned as much during one of our dinner conversations. We have been friends and talked and written one another regularly ever since, but even much more so after we both lost our best friend when Lee died in 2014. A few years later, it was Don's suggestion, and a total shock to me, that we write a book together. This was well after he had already sworn, he was retired and done with his own writing and had written his last book (*Empire of Sand: The Ehrenberg-Quartzsite-Parker Triangle: Myths, Mistakes, Hard Times and a Few Hard Cases*) in 2015. Soon after our collaborative effort "The Earps Invade Southern California" was published (in July 2020), it was again Don's suggestion, and another shock to me, as I actually was looking forward to taking a break and working on promoting our first book, that we write a second book together. Nearly three years later, that book is now due to be released any day now.

EW: Let's also discuss your late friend, the historian and Earp biographer Lee Silva. What memories do you have of Lee that some readers may not know?

DDH: I thank heaven for Lee Silva; he has had such a tremendous impact on my life (and I know me on his too) and sent it in directions I never could have imagined in my wildest dreams. Things would be totally different for me right now if not for him. He brought so much joy into my (and my family's) life; we did so many exciting things together through the years. First with our wives Mary and Sue, but after Sue's death, just the two us of together, and subsequently with Mary and his new girlfriend Carmen. He supported my writings and research and left me in his will to receive his Wild West archives. One thing your readers may not know is that he left me the manuscripts for his planned future Wyatt Earp volumes. On the day of his death, he was due to be at my house delivering the latest chapter for my review/input and planning to pick up research materials that I had for him from my collection for his next Wyatt Earp book volume.

Because he lived at home alone, he was always concerned that he would one day die there, and no one would know about it for months. As it turned out, that couldn't be further from the truth, and I pretty much know exactly when he died down to the minute. Just preceding his death, he had taken a phone call from Greg Lalire who was the editor of *Wild West* Magazine, and another close friend of Lee's, who appears to have been the last person to speak to him. He was then heading off to my house, and when he didn't arrive, we sent someone there to check on him and they found him on the stairs in his home, apparently just about to leave the house. For those who may be interested, I wrote a long article (~14 pages) about how we met, our friendship, and some of the great times we had together, for the Wild West History Association *Journal* of October 2014, a few months after Lee's death. Included is the time we (along with Mary and Sue) attended Lee's good friend, actor Hugh O'Brian's (Wyatt Earp in the 1950s TV show), birthday party together, and sang Happy Birthday to him (along with his celebrity friends including Pat Boone, Marty Ingels, Shirley Jones, and Sammy's wife Altovise Davis), at his home in Beverly Hills.

EW: As you enjoy retirement what other projects do you have on the horizon?

DDH: Yeah; there's *a lot* going on. Don and I have now completed our second book together and it has been picked up by a major publisher. It should be out soon. It is titled Tombstone, Arizona Mystique, and is a totally new take on Tombstone and its ramifications on the rest of the world through the years. You won't believe how influential that town has been on all of our lives; but you will after reading our book.

Don and I have also been working on a series of provocative articles, relating to the book, for publication in Western magazines coinciding with its release.

EW: Any sage advice for newer historians and writers entering the field now or in the future?

DDH: The best part of this whole journey for me, and my family, has been the great friends we have made along the way and the camaraderie. I am a collector of western memorabilia, and a few years back started a Facebook page called the "Wild West Collectors," where about 4000 intense fellow aficionados gather to share their collections and knowledge with one another. It has been very rewarding, and a lot of my close friends and fellow authors/historians/collectors are members and communicate there. That's what I would suggest to those new in the field. Join a group and make friends with other enthusiasts with similar interests and go to the places where history happened together. It will motivate you to keep digging deeper and deeper for the whole story, not just the one which appears in the books. My wife Mary and I, and our children at a very young age, have been to countless historic sites together (family vacations), and it makes it so real when you can actually stand in the footsteps of those who made history before you. Also, if possible, find a special one-in-a-million mentor, like Lee Silva or Don Chaput, as I so fortunately did (lightning certainly struck twice for me) early on. They will point you in the right direction and make certain you don't stumble along the way. Priceless

B.J. Hollars, author of *Go West Young Man: A Father and Son Rediscover America on the Oregon Trail*, among others, is the recipient of the Truman Capote Prize for Literary nonfiction, the Anne B. and James B. McMillian Prize, a 2022 silver medal from the Midwest Book Awards, and more. He is an associate professor of English at the University of Wisconsin-Eau Claire.

EW (Erik Wright): Your new book, *Go West, Young Man: A Father and Son Rediscover America on the Oregon Trail* (Bison Books, 2021), takes a fresh approach to the westward migration story. What inspired this project?

BJH (B.J. Hollars): The truth is the idea came to me as I was sitting in a church pew on Christmas Eve 2017. My son and the rest of the children's choir were singing a rather offkey rendition of "We Three Kings" and when they got to the lyrics, "Westward leading, still proceeding, guide us to Thy perfect light," I sort of just seized upon the idea of a westward trip. Over the course of the year, I'd grown increasingly despondent by the role technology seemed to have in my life. I spent so much time scrolling, and swiping, and clicking my way through my days that I began to realize that I was losing precious time with my son. I wanted to take us to a place beyond cell phone reception, and the west seemed as good a place as any. It felt like a chance to escape some of our 21st century problems, or at least trade them in to learn more about 19th century problems.

But beyond all that, I chose the Oregon Trail because it serves as such a vital illustration of the story of United States' founding and growth. To understand America today, we need to understand the realities of this 23-year period between 1846 and 1869, when 400,000 emigrants traveled west, and 65,000 or so perished along the way. And let's not forget the adverse effects wrought upon indigenous people because of this journey. Westward expansion caused both human and cultural casualties. But if we shy away from this history, then we aren't giving ourselves a fair crack at striving toward a more just country today. I wanted my son to see the beauty of this country, but I wanted him to understand its darkness, too. In learning its full history, I'm hopeful that he might join every American in working toward building that better world.

EW: Your book chronicles a 2,500-mile road trip with your then six-year-old son, Henry. Talk about that experience.

BJH: Where to begin? I usually tell folks that it was the best two weeks of my life. And that is true. But beyond that glorious uninterrupted time together is a larger story related to parents' interactions with their children. In June of 2018, when we struck out on this trip, I was still pretty "golden" in the eyes of my son. Three years later, I'm probably a little less "golden." We still love each other of course, but we are no longer quite the same people we were at that moment in time. He's a big kid now, and he understands the world without my constant commentary. I suppose that should make me proud. But the difficulty of watching our children grow is that they don't just grow up, they grow away. Just a smidge. But still, more than I'd probably like.

What made this experience great is that we took this journey at a perfect moment in both of our lives. We shared the same wide-eyed wonder. He marveled at seeing the West for the first time, and I marveled at watching him marvel.

EW: Did your son enjoy the trip and how much of the history did he grasp?

BJH: Thankfully, Henry still thinks it was the best trip ever. It probably didn't hurt that I plied him with ice cream and more fast food than his mother would have liked. But he earned it. Over the course of those two weeks, Henry joined me in conducting around 15 or 20 interviews with trail experts. Additionally, some days we drove 300+ miles and took part in all sorts of impromptu interviews, too. It was grueling for a 6-year-old. Frankly, it was grueling for a 34-year-old, too. Nothing like what the emigrants experienced, of course, but grueling, nonetheless.

Henry grasped more of the history than I expected. He didn't retain everything he read on placards or at the museums, but when we spoke to experts at Fort Laramie, or Fort Kearny, or at Tamástslikt Cultural Institute he retained what he was told. I cannot fully express my gratitude to all the folks who took time to share their stories with us. Those were the stories that stuck. Those were the lessons we'll both long remember.

EW: What did the trip mean to you as a father?

BJH: I spent years writing this book, yet I've never had the courage to face this question directly. I suppose the trip revealed to me the best version of myself. The best version of both of us, really. If you read the book, you'll see that we had plenty of trouble along the way. But all that trouble somehow brought us closer together.

When I'm having a hard day as a parent, I think back to the night we camped by that creek in Montpelier, Idaho, or the time we climbed to the top of Independence Rock. And I remind myself that we can't be perfect parents all the time, but occasionally, we come close. The trip taught me a little about grace. And a lot about striving toward becoming that better person.

EW: Many sections of the western trails are still largely remote and untouched, but how has the landscape changed since the era of the first westward migrants?

BJH: Well, I'll tell you one thing: there are far more McDonald's these days! Of course, the geologists and trail scholars could answer this question far better than I could, but in my own humble observations, I noted a landscape that was at once unchanged and dramatically changed. There were some stretches of highway along the Platte River where we saw nothing, but railroad tracks off to our left. Occasionally, we would pass a small farming community with a few grain silos alongside those tracks. Sometimes we would pass a yellow sign that just said "Free Range" with a picture of a cow. But other times we would find ourselves caught in traffic jams outside of a city like Portland Oregon, where the skyscrapers loomed forever.

Every time we entered a city, our spirits dropped. We knew what cities looked like, and this was a chance to revel in the landscape. We loved spreading out the tarp, and setting up the tent, and wading up to our knees in the coldest streams we could find. Those were the moments when we could hear the echoes of history most clearly.

EW: Your book deals specifically with the Oregon Trail which is arguably the most famous of the western overland trails. Why is this history still relevant today?

BJH: What a fantastic question. The truth is, so many people of my generation know terribly little about the trail. And what they do know, they mostly learned from the Oregon trail computer game of our youth. We all remember the game's catch phrases— "Don't die of dysentery," and "You better ford the river!"— but the history runs so much deeper than a computer game. I interviewed one of the game's creators, and I think he would agree.

One of the goals of this book was to try to educate readers on the larger Oregon Trail story. History is so much more than names and dates and routes on a map, and I wanted to highlight the personal stories of both emigrants and the indigenous people who called the West home.

Of course, I came to this topic from a place of great humility but learning these stories—and trying to amplify these stories—was one of the honors of my life. I suppose this is the long way of saying that the Oregon Trail matters for the same reason that every square inch of the United States matters: because the land tells a story if we listen.

EW: The Oregon Trail covers half of the country. Is there one place along that vastness that stands out to you in terms of importance or personal meaning? If so, where and for what reason?

BJH: The place that holds the most meaning for me is the grave of Joel Hembree, which is located somewhere in Converse County, Wyoming. A man named Randy Brown accompanied Henry and me to the grave, which is also the site where 6-year-old Joel was run over by a wagon wheel and died in July of 1843. Bringing my own 6-year-old to pay his respects to the 6-year-old who passed away en route to the Willamette Valley was a soul-shaking experience. It was one of those wake-up calls. A reminder that every day is a gift. And that we all only get so many of them.

In terms of Oregon Trail history, Joel Hembree's modest grave likely wouldn't make any historians' "must see" list. But for us, it felt like hallowed ground. It personalized the experience. It connected us to those who came before.

EW: What do you hope your son got out of this trip? How did his experience in seeing the western landscapes unfold before his eyes compare to those children who saw the trail as overland migrants?

BJH: I suppose my greatest hope is that my son will continue to hold tight to this journey's lessons for the rest of his days. I hope that one day he will tell his own children about the time his dad buckled him into the car on the last day of kindergarten and drove him 2500 miles across the country to understand the country more fully. Of course, our experience doesn't hold a candle to what the emigrants experienced all those years ago. Or what the indigenous people experienced. But I think all our stories are linked by our shared love of family. That's one piece of humankind's story that transcends past, present, and future.

Daniel J. Burge is the associate editor of the Register of the Kentucky Historical Society and the coordinator of the society's Research Fellowship Program. He holds a Ph.D. from the University of Alabama, and his work has been published in the *Journal of the Early Republic, Western Historical Quarterly, Pacific Historical Review, Southwestern Historical Quarterly,* and *Journal of the Gilded Age and Progressive Era*. His first book is the celebrated *A Failed Vision of Empire: The Collapse of Manifest Destiny, 1845-1872*.

EW (Erik Wright): Your new book, *A Failed Vision of Empire: The Collapse of Manifest Destiny, 1845-1872,* takes a unique perspective on westward expansion. Let's first discuss the theory behind Manifest Destiny. Who first coined that phrase and why is the idea so deeply rooted in American beliefs?

DJB (Daniel J. Burge): There is some dispute about who coined the phrase "manifest destiny" because it appeared first in a magazine called the *Democratic Review* in an unsigned article. Most historians agree that there were two possible authors of the anonymous article and most seem to think that the phrase was coined by John L. O'Sullivan (who frequently wrote for the *Democratic Review*). We might never know, as nobody claimed credit for inventing the phrase (but I suspect it was O'Sullivan because we have him on record in a later letter using "manifest destiny" again).

After its first appearance in 1845, the phrase found its way into popular culture and later into the history books. Popular papers such as the *New York Herald* and the *New York Times* frequently discussed the relevance of manifest destiny and its possible fulfillment. Beginning in the early twentieth century historians would begin using the phrase as a way to explain American expansion, labelling the decade of the 1840s the "era of manifest destiny." So, in a sense, manifest destiny has lived a double life: it was frequently invoked in the nineteenth century and from the twentieth century onwards it has been described as a core American belief.

EW: You argue that our traditional views of Manifest Destiny were not a singular and successful national movement, but rather something that was widely contested and disputed among politicians and other expansionists. Can you elaborate on this?

DJB: A central argument I make in the book is that we have fundamentally misunderstood the meaning of manifest destiny. Most historians today would define manifest destiny as the belief that the United States was destined to expand from coast-to-coast. Many argue that manifest destiny was popular and that it was a sort of foundational American belief of the 1840s. What I found when doing research for this book, however, was that Americans living in the nineteenth century did not use manifest destiny as a synonym for western expansion. When nineteenth-century Americans spoke of manifest destiny they referred to continental domination, to the belief that the United States would acquire the continent of North America. It was not necessarily an "east-to-west" ideology, but rather looked north (to Canada), south (to Mexico), and east (to islands such as Cuba).

What I try to show in each chapter of the book is how Americans living in the nineteenth century debated manifest destiny and how the ideology eventually faded away in the mid-1870s. I'll be the first to admit that it's something of a controversial argument, but I think the sources back it up.

EW: What was the Oregon Question?

DJB: One problem with writing a book is that portions are eventually cut out, so I don't really talk a lot about the Oregon Question (although I did in earlier versions). Essentially, the Oregon Question was a dispute between the United States and Great Britain over the boundary in the Pacific Northwest. Beginning in the 1840s, both Great Britain and the United States increasingly sought to gain control of the region, which threatened to bring the two nations into a war. The election of James K. Polk in 1844 seemed to point the way to an eventual war between the two powers.

The Oregon Question sort of loomed in the 1840s, although both sides later worked things out. There was a great deal of bluster from Democratic politicians, but in the end Polk and others decided it was wiser to patch things up with Britain and compromise on the boundary, instead of fighting another war.

EW: Regardless of these disparate views was America destined to stretch from the Atlantic to the Pacific?

DJB: This is a tricky question, but it is one that I've thought quite a bit about. We know the shape that America eventually takes, so it's somewhat easy today to look back and go: "of course the United States was going to expand from the Atlantic to the Pacific." What I hope readers will remember is that Americans living in the nineteenth century envisioned many possible configurations of what the boundaries of the U.S. would be. Many were convinced that it would include Canada and a larger chunk of Mexico than the U.S. took in 1848. U.S. Grant thought it would include the Dominican Republic (and it nearly did).

Let me put this a different way. For a moment, imagine the U.S. does not claim the Rio Grande after the annexation of Texas and so the U.S. does not fight the U.S.-Mexican War (it still annexes Texas, but the annexation does not lead to a boundary dispute and war). Even without the U.S.-Mexican War, the United States would still have been a continental nation, one that stretched from the Atlantic to the Pacific, because the U.S. would have still laid claim to Montana, Wyoming, Idaho, Oregon, Washington. The United States, of course, would not then include what we consider to be the Southwest, but it would still have ports on the Pacific Coast and would be a continental nation. Was the United States destined to do that? I would argue no, but I do think the majority of Americans would have accepted ports along the Pacific as necessary by the mid-1850s, even if the U.S. did not lay claim to the stretch in between.

EW: What was the contemporary view from outside America during this period of expansion? Were other countries and our allies supportive or critical of such ambitious goals?

DJB: The nineteenth century is so interesting because the United States does not have "allies" in the sense that we think of allies today. Great Britain, France, Spain, and Mexico were certainly determined not to let the United States expand and they resisted with varying degrees of success. Granted, Mexico loses the U.S.-Mexican War, but proponents of manifest destiny were unable to seize all of Mexico, as they desired. Great Britain proved a bit more successful, as it managed to prevent the United States from gobbling up Canada (and worked to blunt the U.S. drive into Central America).

In a sense, I do think Great Britain underestimated the ability of the United States to expand westward and failed to prevent the United States from acquiring Texas (and then the rest of the Southwest in the U.S.-Mexican War). It bears mentioning, I think, that Great Britain could not have known that the United States would rise to become a dominant power. France understood the importance of western expansion and tried to establish its own empire in Mexico during the U.S. Civil War. By the mid-nineteenth century, most European colonial powers were realizing how difficult it was to establish a hold in North America and so it's difficult to say whether or not they could have prevented U.S. expansion if they had simply committed to it.

EW: What hurdles did contemporary Americans face during this period of Westward Expansion both in terms of physical obstacles and geopolitical issues?

DJB: I'll get to some of the physical obstacles in the next question, but I think we can overlook how important political and sectional obstacles were. Prior to the Civil War, the issue of slavery came into every single debate over U.S. expansion, as folks debated whether or not "the West" would be open to slavery or not. I think most people are somewhat familiar with those debates.

What I try to highlight throughout the book is the extent to which political divisions hindered expansion. Whigs did not think it was necessary to go to war with Mexico (and firmly stood against the acquisition of more territory). After the Civil War, the parties flip on the issue of expansion and when U.S. Grant tries to annex the

Dominican Republic, Democrats oppose it (and manage to convince enough Republicans to block the annexation). Put differently, I think we need to understand how contested the process of western expansion was and that different groups of people had different plans for the West. It's not as if folks simply agreed on everything. In the nineteenth century, partisan divisions ran deep.

EW: What roles did the Overland Trails and later, the First Transcontinental Railroad, play in this expansion?

DJB: Both the Overland Trails and the Transcontinental Railroad were pivotal to the process of western expansion. Any time that you write a book, you have to leave out certain details and it's even trickier when you are trying to tackle a long period of time (as opposed to a single war or a single decade). Because my book focuses on debates over the acquisition of territory, I spend little time on how the areas that were acquired were incorporated into the United States. The book I always recommend, for those interested, is John D. Unruh's classic *The Plains Across*, as he does such a good job with the trails.

EW: Talk about the development of this book. How did you first conceive of it as a worthy project?

DJB: I could talk about this for quite a while. Originally, I was interested in looking at folks who were speaking out against manifest destiny, because I thought most historians had ignored them. That became the topic of my dissertation, as I tried to sketch out how individuals challenged manifest destiny. The more I researched and wrote, however, the more I came to realize that there was a lot more to the story than I had been taught. Manifest destiny always seemed so simple in history textbooks, so I eventually realized I had a pretty good topic. I do always like to acknowledge, as well, that other historians have made similar arguments about the failure of manifest destiny. Yet their works tend to focus on the 1840s and early 1850s, while I stretch mine all the way to the Grant administration.

It still took a long time before I found my central argument: that manifest destiny had very little to do with what we can call "western expansion." Historians since the 1920s have used the phrase "manifest destiny" to refer to the U.S. push westward (Texas, New Mexico, California, etc.), but that is not at all how Americans in the nineteenth century saw it. The more I worked through the sources, the more I came to understand that nineteenth-century Americans defined manifest destiny as the conquest of the continent of North America and always spoke of it as involving the acquisition of Canada, Cuba, and Mexico. It was only later that academic historians redefined manifest destiny to refer to western expansion (what I end up calling "the myth of manifest destiny").

In other words, I would say it has been a process. I knew I had hit on an interesting project while I was a graduate student at Alabama, but a lot changed in my interpretation as I worked on revising the dissertation to turn it into a book. It was only then that I realized I was not just writing a history of the opponents of manifest destiny but that I was arguing that manifest destiny was not popular and that it was unfulfilled.

Bradley G. Courtney is known as Prescott, Arizona's "Whiskey Row Historian," Courtney has written books, articles, and lectured extensively on the Arizona city he calls home. Among his books are *The Whiskey Row Fire of 1900* and *True Tales of Prescott*. His other work has appeared in *True West* magazine and *The Tombstone Epitaph*.

EW (Erik Wright): Talk about your interest in the history of Prescott, Arizona, and Western history. Where did it begin?

BGC (Bradley G. Courtney): I am a southwestern Michigan farm boy who moved to Arizona in 1981 after taking a teaching job on the Navajo Reservation. I thought I'd try it out for a year because, perhaps because my mother was Native American, that culture, and the West in general, intrigued me. However, I fell in love with the people and the land up there and stayed for twelve years. For six years I was a Colorado River boat pilot, a beyond dreams job that also kept me there. But for family reasons, I moved to and lived in Phoenix for nineteen years but, not being a city person, would often come up to Prescott to get away. I then moved there after retiring from teaching in 2011. I loved my new hometown and wanted to learn all about its history but discovered that a definitive history of its Whiskey Row, which I was enamored with, did not exist. I took that as a sign, and that has been my mission ever since.

EW: Why is Prescott important to the history of Arizona as both a territory and a state?

BGC: As many know, Prescott was the capital of Arizona Territory 1864-1867, and 1877-1889. That and the fact that Prescott is near the geographical center of Arizona made it a go-to place, if not just to pass through, during those years. When I was researching for my first book, *Prescott's Original Whiskey Row*, I was astounded at the breadth and width of Prescott's history and concluded it was the heart and soul of historical Arizona. Now it's not only a thriving, vibrant town, but a popular tourist destination for people from all over the world.

EW: Was Prescott known to be a violent town like some others in Arizona like Tombstone and Tucson?

BGC: Prescott often had a reputation as being a peaceful, law-abiding town. The truth, however, is that it required a ton of taming to earn that standing. When Prescott lost its territorial capital status in 1867, it seemed to lose its identity for a while. In 1869, the editor of the local newspaper complained, "Our once quiet village is getting to be a regular Pandemonium. Drunken men quarrel, fight, and shoot." Truly, you can't have a row named after whiskey smack-dab in the middle of town, and not have violence therein! It required some strong lawmen along the way to gain order. Still, Drew Desmond and I wrote the book *Murder & Mayhem in Prescott* and found that we had to really pick and choose chapters, there was so much material to choose from. We wound up with sixteen chapters but could easily write a *Murder & Mayhem in Prescott, II*.

EW: How did the Great Prescott Fire of 1900 affect the development of the town?

BGC: It was *the* pivotal event in Prescott's history. The question "Do we continue this dream called Prescott? Or do we throw in the towel?" were very real. To a person, the answer was "We will rebuild bigger and better." And those hearty pioneers did just that! Prescott legend Morris Goldwater claimed that "The great fire of 1900 was the best thing that ever happened to Prescott." That statement typified the town's pioneer spirit, and we are the benefactors of it today.

EW: Talk about Whiskey Row. What is it and how is it remembered today by both scholars and visitors.

BGC: When early Prescott was being established, saloons—the social hubs of the West—went up as fast and sometimes faster than mercantile stores, etc., and buildings from which to run the government. Over time a row of them, to the chagrin of some (Prescott's first church building did not appear until 1875), formed along Montezuma Street. I like to call Whiskey Row the "Allen Street" of Prescott. As I mentioned, up until my work the Row had not been given much scholarly attention. It was rife with hearsay legends that some, unfortunately, I've had the displeasure of debunking. But as they say, truth is often more interesting than fiction, and that has proven to be overwhelmingly true with Whiskey Row. Today, visitors feel like they are stepping back in time. That is especially true regarding Prescott's iconic Palace Restaurant and Saloon.

EW: Your latest book *True Tales of Prescott* was co-authored with Drew Desmond. Can you talk a little about this book and some of the interesting stories you uncovered?

BGC: Drew is a relentless story pursuer, and he focused on the true tales outside of the Row, while I of course focused on them. We both have stated that it was a very pleasant book to write. My favorite story on my part was the famous "baby on the bar" story, which a legend formed around and was told for over seven decades but was quite different than the true story, which was fun to dig out. The legend would make a better movie, but the true tale proves more interesting, and enlightening. All of Drew's stories are great, but the one that especially caused me to go "Wow!" was a chapter entitled, "Smoking Marijuana was a Community Event." Even the famed scientist, Percival Lowell, came down to Prescott from Flagstaff for a smoking event sponsored by the chamber!

EW: Can you describe your life as a historian who writes, lectures, and gives tours?

BGC: I was a middle-school teacher for thirty-one years, but my passion (and education) has always been history. Becoming a full-time historian had long been my goal and dream. To be the fellow who researches and writes Whiskey Row history, well, I could not have even dreamed that possibility up! The response has been overwhelming; there seems to be a longing for it from Prescottonians, and even from outsiders. My lectures are often standing room only. And my tours have seen as many as fifty people at a time.

EW: What projects do you plan to work on in 2023? Will they be focused on Prescott?

BGC: I am glad you asked! After *True Tales of Prescott*, I began working on making into a book my master's thesis, which was on the last five months of the Geronimo Campaign. But the desire to finish the telling of Whiskey Row history has proven much too strong. I am extremely excited about my latest book project. I am currently calling it *The Prescott/Tombstone Connection*. Along with my friend, Prescott Constable Ron Williams (who proudly serves in the same elected post that Virgil Earp held in 1878-79), I have discovered there is a fascinating story to tell stemming from more than just the fact that the Earps and Doc Holliday and those associated with them were in Prescott before heading down to Tombstone, where they found immortality. After that, I will work on the history of Whiskey Row from 1902 up to the present day. It's really rewarding because it all feels groundbreaking, because no one has discovered and published a full and true history of the Row before!

Larry D. Ball is Professor Emeritus at Arkansas State University in Jonesboro and the author of several books on the West. His most recent, *Tom Horn: In Life and Legend*, was met with high acclaim. Other works include his celebrated studies on the Wham paymaster robbery and the U.S. Marshals and sheriffs of the desert southwest during the 19th century.

EW (Erik Wright): How did you first become interested in Western History?

LDB (Larry D. Ball): As a boy growing up in rural eastern Arkansas, I spent much time with my grandfather, a retired country schoolteacher. He told me stories from history which whetted my appetite for more. I also began to read western and adventure magazines to pass the time. Such magazines as True West and Frontier Times introduced me to many writers of non-fiction, such as Father Stanley, Ed Bartholomew, and Glenn Shirley. In the 1950s, I began to purchase their books, although $3.50 or $5.00 was difficult to come by. I began to wonder about their sources and to hope that I might gain access to them some day.

EW: How did that interest evolve into a career?

LDB: As a freshman at Arkansas State University (Jonesboro) in 1957, I began to feel at home almost immediately and hoped to make college teaching a career. Many years were required to prepare myself, and I did not complete my graduate work at the University of Colorado (Boulder) until 1970. However, I was able to continue my interest in the west and selected the subject of the United States marshals of New Mexico and Arizona territories for my Ph.D. dissertation subject. In order to complete the dissertation, my professors, Robert Athearn and Clifford P. Westermeier, emphasized the necessity of using primary sources when possible. This requirement took me to the National Archives in Washington, D. C., and various historical societies in the Southwest. This training set me off on an enjoyable research and publication career.

EW: Talk about your early work on the U. S. Marshals. Did you have previous authors to lean on for your research or were you breaking new territory?

LDB: My choice of the United States Marshals as a subject for serious study was something of an accident. I recall the day that I approached Professor Athearn, who helped me select a dissertation subject, with a list of possible topics, among them the frontier county sheriffs, U. S. marshals, and one or two more. He immediately recommended the marshals. At the time, I knew very little about the U. S. marshals. Since they were presidential appointees, the popular works on western characters, such as Wyatt Earp and Bat Masterson, said little about the marshals. Earp was a sometime deputy U. S. marshal, but he could hardly aspire to the more exalted position of U. S. marshal for federal district court. My learning experience had just begun. As a consequence, I found myself breaking new ground and learning on the job as I explored Department of Justice material in the National Archives.

EW: You have written largely about law enforcement and banditry in the southwest. How have your interests in these subjects matured over the years?

LDB: My appreciation of the achievements of law enforcement in the Southwest has increased over the years. When I began my studies in a serious way in the 1960s, I accepted the prevailing notion that the frontier was a very violent place and that there was very little, if any, law enforcement. The popular works of Walter Noble Burns and Stuart Lake were somewhat misleading in that they concentrated on men who were part-time lawmen and usually members of the frontier sporting crowd. While I still agree that there were outbreaks of violence, my feeling is that the majority of settlers were law abiding people. After all, most pioneers went west to seek their fortunes, and they were willing to work for a better future. They were optimistic, and this optimism was apparent in their slow, if sometimes uneven, establishment of law and order by the early 1900s. I found that the men who filled critical positions—U. S. marshals and county sheriffs— were largely nameless and obscure. They were members of offices that had a cumulative impact on law enforcement in the long term. I hope that this idea is apparent in my approach to both the U. S. marshals and the county sheriffs. I have tried to emphasize this collective nature of law enforcement on the frontier rather than simply narrate the stories of individual lawmen.

EW: As an academic have you faced challenges in bringing legitimacy to the stories of frontier violence?

LDB: As an academic I have probably faced no more challenges to my particular interests than other scholars. It is true that within academia there has always been resistance to the "wild west" or "cowboy and Indians" approach to frontier history, but I have always had colleagues with similar interest in law enforcement in the West and I hope that we have a respected place in the scholarly world.

EW: Describe your research and writing process.

LDB: I find that one research project generally grows out of, or springs from, the proceeding one. Of course, there has to be a starting point. It was my good fortune that professors Athearn and Westermeier turned my attention to the U. S. marshal's office on the frontier. It was sort of logical for me to turn next to sheriff's office since these county officers cooperated closely with federal lawmen. I have also made some effort to demonstrate the participation of the U. S. Army and territorial militias in law enforcement. Even my last work—the story of Tom Horn—does not venture too far from this theme.

    I have always counted myself lucky to have lived in an era where the study of the history of the American West was popular and both the federal government and individual states have supported libraries and archives. These research institutions make various collections of documents readily available. I have also been fortunate in that my professors at the University of Colorado emphasized the basics in research methodology—search out your places of research in advance; have some notion as to the collections you want to see; and take notes in a uniform fashion. Of course, copy machines and digitization of sources have made research so much easier but, at the same time, have added some complications to this process. I have always enjoyed research and uncovering new sources much more than writing. I find that organizing my notes and writing is often difficult. I envy writers who have the gift of composing only one draft. Three or four drafts are usually required before I reach some sort of satisfaction.

EW: What lessons have you learned from your own career or mentors that you would like to see passed down?

LDB: I think there are certain rules or practices in research that every writer should pursue. A healthy skepticism in regard to the reliability of sources is helpful. Is your source able to tell the truth? Is your source willing to tell the truth? A uniform method of taking and organizing notes is also helpful. Yet, I admit that I often lose or misplace critical notes and have to stop and search them out. I also believe that attendance at historical conventions is important. Although it is easy for me to play the hermit and isolate myself in my ivory tower, associating with fellow students of the west is very important.

EW: What projects are you currently researching?

LDB: My work on Tom Horn led me out of the Southwest and into Wyoming where the U. S. marshals encountered problems similar to their counterparts in Arizona and New Mexico. I am currently working with John W. Davis, a veteran attorney and keen student of Wyoming history, on the facts and legend of Hole-in-the-Wall. I also hope to revise and enlarge my biography of Elfego Baca.

Linda Wommack is a long-time contributor to *True West* magazine, *The Tombstone Epitaph*, *Wild West* magazine, the WWHA *Journal*, and others. She is recognized as a leading authority of Colorado history for which she has written several books including, *Murder in the Mile High City: The First Hundred Years*, *Growing Up with the Wild Bunch: The Story of Pioneer Legend Josie Bassett*, and *From Sand Creek to Summit Springs: Colorado's Indian Wars* which was the winner of a Will Rogers gold medallion in 2023.

EW (Erik Wright): Talk about growing up in Colorado. Did that have an influence on your history of the West?

LW (Linda Wommack): I am a native Coloradoan. My parents loved history and would often recount Colorado history stories during Sunday drives through the mountains. I became hooked on history at a very young age.

EW: You are associated with all the major western history publications including the WWHA, *The Tombstone Epitaph*, *True West,* and *Wild West* magazines. How do you juggle your different assignments?

LW: It has been an absolute privilege and honor to write for such great publications for over 25 years now. I have learned to be very focused and very disciplined in my research and writing. As it turns out, I work better that way!

EW: As a woman in a male-dominated field what challenges have you faced over the course of your career?

LW: I try not to look at it that way. I have always worked hard to prove myself through my research and findings. Working with knowledgeable folks in the field, male or female is a great learning experience and very rewarding on many levels.

EW: Your most recent book, *Growing Up with the Wild Bunch: The Story of Pioneer Legend Josie Bassett* tells the history of a largely forgotten frontier figure. Who was Josie Bassett and why did you choose to pen a biography of her?

LW: I have been researching the Bassett family of Brown's Park Colorado off and on for over 30 years. I wrote the first biography of Ann Bassett in 2018. I had so much information and a fascination for Josie that I decided to write her biography. Both women were extraordinary for their times and deserve to have their true story told. True is the operative word here for Josie tended to be a braggart and exaggerate quite a bit. The book wrestles that apart and reveals the real Josie Bassett through my years of research.

EW: Why does the Wild Bunch Gang continue to grip the world's interest?

LW: I think it is because they are so elusive. No one knows for sure what happened to Butch and Sundance or Etta Place for that matter. It is a subject that both fascinates and aggravates researchers and readers alike. Who were those guys?

EW: Another recent book of yours, *Murder in the Mile High City: The First Hundred Years*, is an exhaustive study of murder in Denver, Colorado. Describe your research into this project and how you opted for the murder cases you profiled.

LW: It sounds strange, but researching murder stories for this book was absolutely incredible. Every time I thought I had the strangest tale of murder, a stranger one came along. Long hours at the Denver Public Library, the Denver Police Museum archives and newspaper accounts revealed a treasure trove of information.

EW: Was there a favorite or particularly interesting murder case from that book you'd like to share?

LW: From the story of 12-year-old Anton Woode, the youngest prisoner sent to the state penitentiary, to the mob wars and murder in 1930s Denver, the assassinations of not one but two priests at the altar of Denver's Catholic churches or the horrific strangulations in Denver's red-light district, each story is riveting.

EW: How do you maintain your interest and passion for history and writing?

LW: It is a passion. Since childhood I have truly loved history. Research is my favorite part. There is nothing more exciting, invigorating or satisfying as a historian when something new has been discovered or one's theory is finally proven with documentation.

EW: What book projects do you have slated for the future?

LW: I am always doing interesting research. I just completed *Indian Wars of Colorado* [*From Sand Creek to Summit Springs: Colorado's Indian Wars*] and am currently working on two women history related books.

EW: Finally, what advice do you offer to the next generation of Western historians and especially those young girls out there who may look to writers like you as an example?

LW: Learn all you can. Ask the experts in the field. Read, research and research some more. Stay true to yourself and your values.

Mike Mihaljevich is a noted photographer and Tombstone historian. He has written for the WWHA *Journal* and presented his research titled, "An Epidemic of Shooting: Ordinance # 9 and the Truth About Gun Control in Tombstone" at the annual Tombstone Territory Rendezvous held each fall in Tombstone, Arizona. He is currently working on his first book tentatively to be released in 2024.

EW (Erik Wright): Talk about the modern West. Where is it and what does it mean to you?

MM (Mike Mihaljevich): The West means so many things to different people. I tend to see the whole gamut from unprecedented opportunity and salvation to unchecked greed and broken morals. I see the modern West as a continuing story of how it was opened up 200 years ago and what we've done with it since - for better or worse. I travel 30,000 miles over its roadways every year. It takes very little imagination to look out into the open to see it as the frontier it once was. It's a special place to me - the stage on which American mythology played out. I'm honored to spend time there and to become more intimately acquainted.

EW: Can you still find traces of the old west (or even the ancient west) in your travels?

MM: Absolutely. My travel allows me to hunt the scattered bones of the young West. I've seen the remote banks of the Red River worn by millions of cattle driven to Kansas. I've seen the footings of the Dale Creek bridge on the Transcontinental Railroad. I know what it looks like to crest the hill Fettermen's men climbed on their way to abrupt defeat. I've seen the confluence of the Missouri and Yellowstone where the Corps of Discovery had a decision to make. Most importantly seeing the vast distances between allows me to appreciate the scale and challenge of western conquest. There are many lasting relics. Beyond physical remains, I am encouraged by how many places embrace their western roots and how many people travel considerable distances to get a taste of it. I regularly see reinvigorated historic buildings, events and commerce centered around this history. This gives me hope that western enthusiasm will endure.

EW: What led to your interest in photography?

MM: I tend to respond to things that challenge me. Early on I was consistently disappointed to realize photographs I had taken didn't transmit the same feeling of seeing the scene in person. Problem solving this became the challenge. I never want to show someone a photograph of a place that moved me and have to explain "it was really cool… just trust me". I want the photograph to directly communicate the experience of seeing it in person - or as close as possible. Simple in concept, difficult in practice. I've been fortunate to unravel that riddle and have measures of humbling success doing it. Photographs can convey messages that words can't. It also documents ever-changing people and places. In the historical context, that makes it very valuable.

EW: Do you have a favorite place in the west? If so, where is it and why is it so meaningful?

MM: So many places in the West are special to me. One that put a deep mark on me is Fort Union on the Montana/North Dakota border. Fort Union was a private trading post that conducted commerce with many remote native nations of the Northern plains in the early and mid-1800s. The grounds overlooking the historic Missouri are completely unchanged from its operational period. A very extensive archaeological dig was conducted there in the 1990s. Much of what was recovered is on display at the Fort which was masterfully reconstructed on its original footings. I recommend reading George Catlin's writings who candidly described his experience there (and his horseback buffalo hunt that puts "Dances with Wolves" to shame). I also recommend reading "Fort Union and the Upper Missouri Fur Trade" by Barton H. Barbour. After reading both you're prepared for a visit. While there takes a moment to sit inside the trading room amongst the aroma from the original fireplace. Sit on the canon in the west bastion where Catlin painted his subjects. Walk the grounds outside the fort where natives who came from afar camped in peace among their enemies. Then take a moment at the Fort's entrance fronting the Missouri. Marvel at the worn pebbles and rocks in that entrance smoothed by the foot traffic of legends. It is sacred ground representing a fascinating and important segment in western history that is often overlooked.

EW: Let's talk Tombstone. You are a regular at annual Tombstone history gatherings such as the Tombstone Territory Rendezvous. What got you engaged in the history of the Town Too Tough to Die?

MM: My grandfather, a hardworking and proud Pearl Harbor survivor, was in love with western history. It wasn't until he raised his kids and retired in his late 60s that he was able to act on it. He talked grandma into moving from Milwaukee, Wisconsin to Green Valley, Arizona and may have visited Tombstone before he got his toothbrush unpacked. This love was genetically inherited by my father who still watches a western tv show or movie every day and never misses an opportunity to talk about western history. He grew up on a steady diet of western movies and television of the '50s and '60s. By virtue of watching reruns my entire childhood, I grew up on virtually the same. Then in 1993 he took me to see "Tombstone" on the big screen. I asked him endless questions on the ride home, raided our set of encyclopedias when we got back, and listened to the soundtrack on cassette tape until it wore out. Fast forward 20 years, I was living in Tombstone and working hands-on with historic records in the City Archives where I developed an addiction for primary source research to unveil deeper truths the movies vaguely represented. The journey has never left me with tired legs. For the better part of the last decade, I've been working on a project that contributes to the ongoing and expanding Tombstone discussion. I hope to unveil it shortly. There is so much more out there waiting to be uncovered.

EW: You have many photographs that include animals as subjects such as bison, elk, and bighorn sheep. Have you ever been charged or attacked while photographing them?

MM: One method of improving my photography is learning more about my subjects. This is important for minimizing risk and maximizing opportunities. When you step out of your car and into the mountains, you're agreeing to nature's longstanding rules. You either follow them or pay penalties ranging from bruised ego to injury or death. I have not been charged but have seen it happen to other photographers. Generally, the victim hasn't become educated about their subject or gained respect for their surroundings before putting the camera to their eye. There's always an element of luck, but I find the more respect you have out there the "luckier" you tend to be.

EW: Many of your photographs capture the ethereal spirit of the west. Describe your process for selecting locations or subjects and how long you may wait at a location to capture the perfect image.

MM: I'm predisposed to historically significant locations but am also drawn to landscapes and subjects which epitomize the "West of imagination". I always head out with a plan. But you have to be willing to completely abandon the plan and work with the changing situation around you. Executing a planned shot and being able to work on the fly are two necessary (and very different) skills. In either case I give over to creative visions. Sometimes these are in my mind before I head to a location. Other times they come to me in the moment. I've waited hours, even slept on locations for a week or more trying to get things right. Love for your subject is tested in an exercise like that. Sometimes the perfect shot falls in your lap, other times you have to dig for it. You have to love it both ways. The West is a sacred and magical place to me - one that I can't put to words. If I can take a photograph that inspires that same feeling in others when looking at it, then I've achieved my goal. If I inspire anyone to buy a camera, visit a location, or take an interest in one of the historic subjects, even better.

EW: Have you taken inspiration from earlier frontier photographers like Carleton Watkins or Edward Curtis?

MM: Curtis and Watkins, absolutely. They are Bach and Mozart. I admire them for their subject matter and technical skill. They developed mastery of a laborious (but cutting edge in its time) photographic process. Other greats of influence: William Henry Jackson, Alexander Gardner, Roland Reed, Frederick Monsen, Timothy O'Sullivan, Karl Moon, Arundel Hull, L.A. Huffman, Alfred Hart to name a few. If you were to examine the lives of these men, the places they traveled, and the subjects they photographed, you would be exposed to a significant swatch of western history. Several have proper biographies which I encourage people to read. I'm inspired by other period artists such as Karl Bodmer and Albert Bierstadt. I can't tell you how many times I've said to myself if I can shoot as well as Bierstadt painted, I'd consider myself successful. If anyone is reading this looking up Bierstadt's work on the internet, please commit yourself to seeing at least one in person. It's an experience a screen cannot convey. Like my motive to travel the West, you just have *see* it.

Mike Bell retired from a distinguished career in the United Kingdom's education system. Since then, he has done important research and writing in the Old West field. For decades, he's focused his attention on the Wild Bunch, uncovering little known facts about the gang and its associates—and the men who fought them. Bell, who has a Ph.D. in history, has had articles published by most of the Western publications, including *The Epitaph.* He has written several books with his latest being *Who Are Those Guys? Of Myths and Manhunters: The Union Pacific Bandit Hunters.*

EW (Erik Wright): How and when did your interest in the Old West start?

MB (Mike Bell): Like many people, my interest began in the 1960s. At that time there were only two TV channels in the UK, and most evenings there were Westerns showing on both. Then I became interested in the history behind the fiction. I bought a copy of Paul Hann and James D. Horan's *Pictorial History of the Wild West* and then began building my library. That was in the pre-Internet era, when books from the United States were very expensive and took a very long time to reach the UK.

When I began studying for my doctorate in 1979, I tried to convince my professor to let me do something on banditry in the United States. I even took along a copy of Professor Larry Ball's book on United States Marshals to try to convince him. He said no! But the training stood me in good stead even if the subject matter wasn't exactly what I wanted. And it did take me on my first visit to the United States in 1980 as part of my research– and I just kept coming back.

EW: At what point did you start to focus on the Wild Bunch, and why?

MB: On my 13th birthday in 1969. A friend and I went to see *Butch Cassidy and the Sundance Kid.* Unfortunately, we arrived very late for the showing we had planned to catch, but the usherette said we could go in anyway.
　　So, I saw the end of the movie before the beginning, which spoils the plot a bit. It is a great piece of entertainment but a very poor history, like most movies. But it got me interested in Butch Cassidy and the Wild Bunch.

EW: How much of your research has been done from England, and how much was done in visits to the U.S.?

MB: I first visited Wyoming back in 1986 and since then have made about 30 research trips to the West to visit museums, archives, libraries, and to visit sites where events happened. There is nothing like standing in a muddy field in Wyoming where once the Wild Bunch rode. As the years have gone by, more and more material has become available online as newspapers, photograph collections and archives have been digitized. Also, e-mail communication has made it easier to talk to museums and archives about their collections and get copies of key photographs and documents.

EW: When was this "super posse" created?

MB: The first version of the Bandit Hunters was put together in the summer of 1902 by the Chief of the Wyoming division of the Union Pacific Secret Service, Timothy T. Keliher, under instructions from

Superintendent William Park, and Bill Canada, overall Chief of the Union Pacific Police. Keliher recruited the Bandit Hunters and had a train on standby in Cheyenne and horses and weapons stationed at key points on the line between Cheyenne and Green River – the so-called "bandit belt." So, the Bandit Hunters didn't appear on the scene until two years after the last Wild Bunch train robbery in Wyoming and a year after their train robbery at Wagner, Montana.

The Union Pacific put armed guards on some trains after the June 1899 Wilcox robbery, but that didn't prevent the Tipton robbery in 1900. The combination of armed guards to fight off robbers, and the Bandit Hunters to chase them down seems to have done the trick. But neither the guards nor the Bandit hunters were a standing force. The guards were usually laid off in the winter, when the threat of train robbery waned, and the Bandit Hunters had other jobs as regular lawmen and were there to be called upon if needed.

As the years went by, the formation of the Bandit Hunters was backdated to shortly after the Tipton robbery, and then to just after Wilcox.

EW: Who were the key players in the Bandit Hunters?

MB: Exactly who had the original idea for the Bandit Hunters and the special train is still unclear. E.H. Harriman, William Park, Bill Canada, and Joe Lefors all claimed to have played a part.

Timothy T. Keliher, former Sheriff from North Platte, Nebraska was the key operational player. He was appointed in January 1902 as assistant to Canada – in effect as the head of the Wyoming Division of the U.P. Police. He appointed Grosvenor Arthur Porter, who led the

Bandit Hunters in 1902 and 1903. Porter went on to be a U.S. Marshal in the Indian Territory, Chief of Police in the Canal Zone, and member of the U.S. Secret Service.

Then Kelliher led the Bandit Hunters personally. Deputy United States Marshal Lefors was a key member of the Hunters, as was Union Pacific policeman Tom Meggison. He had been in the posse that killed Flat-Nosed George Currie in 1900.

Scott 'Quick-Shot' Davis was a veteran stagecoach guard who had ridden with the invaders of Johnson County in 1892. He was brought in to buy the Union Pacific horses, the best money could buy. He was helped by Hiram Davis. Not a relative.

Pete Bergerson was a champion rifle shot from Laramie; Frank Spurlock, Silas Funk, Tommy Meggeson, George Pickering, and Cyrus van Sickle were all railroad policemen, while George Hiatt was the foreman of the O-O ranch, who had been part of the Wilcox posse.

EW: In the movie, the super posse is led by an Indian tracker called Lord Baltimore. Was there such a person?

MB: I have found no record of any Indian character being involved with the Bandit Hunters. But there are two facts that might have led William Goldman, scriptwriter for Butch Cassidy and the Sundance Kid, to invent the character. The first is that some of the 1904 photographs appear to show an unnamed Indian. The second is that as part of the publicity for the Bandit Hunters the Union Pacific said they had an arrangement with the Arapaho and Shoshone tribes at Fort Washakie to supply trackers if ever they were needed. I'm still trying to trace the history of the Indian in the photographs.

EW: What's the tie to Buffalo Bill?

MB: He needed a new show. Buffalo Bill was touring in Europe for several years in the early 1900s. When he came back to the United States, he wanted to update his show. He tried to recruit some of the real Bandit Hunters, and some of the men who rode after the Wilcox and Topton train robbers, but they all turned him down. But Bill was a showman. He had a fake train made and added the Bandit Hunters to his 1907-1908 tour.

By that time the real Bandit Hunters had ceased to exist, but the publicity brought by Buffalo Bill's show helped to fuel the myth that they had destroyed the Wild Bunch and were still a force to be reckoned with.

EW: Were the Bandit Hunters successful, at least in deterring train holdups?

MB: They were. While other railroads continued to be hit by train robbers after 1902, the Union Pacific did not suffer another serious train robbery in Wyoming until Bill Carlisle attacked them in 1916, and he was a lone wolf operator.

When the Denver and Rio Grande railroad was robbed at Parachute, Colorado in 1904 one of the bandits was wounded and then killed himself. The railroad police and others believed that the bandits had originally planned to hit the Union Pacific but were deterred by the threat of the Bandit Hunters. The dead man was finally identified as Harvey Logan, better known as Kid Curry. So indirectly the Bandit hunters may have contributed to the death of one of the West's most notorious outlaws and train robbers.

Butch Cassidy and the Sundance Kid left for South America in 1901, but part of the purpose of the publicity campaign for the Bandit Hunters was to ensure that if they ever came back, they would think twice before hitting the U.P.

Matt Fitzsimons, a San Diego-based writer, historian, and filmmaker, uncovers a fascinating and heartbreaking story of southwestern slavery in his debut book *The Counterfeiters of Bosque Redondo: Slavery, Silver, and the U.S. War Against the Navajo Nation*.

EW (Erik Wright): Your new book, *The Counterfeiters of Bosque Redondo: Slavery, Silver, and the U.S. War Against the Navajo Nation*, is a beautifully written history of a forgotten and tragic chapter in American history. Can you tell readers what your book is about?

MF (Matt Fitzsimons): Thank you for that great introduction. The book takes a fresh look at the forced exile of the Navajo Nation, often referred to as the Long Walk of the Navajo. In the 1860s, the U.S Army rounded up thousands of men, women, and children, and imprisoned them hundreds of miles from home at a desolate camp called Bosque Redondo. This is the story of how those families ended up there, and how, against all odds, they managed to get back home.

EW: Who was Herrero Delgadito?

MF: He's widely credited as the first Diné (Navajo) silversmith. Among the Diné, he's usually remembered by the name Atsidí Sání, or "Old Pounder." He was also a medicine man, a brother of the great orator Barboncito, and the first major headman to surrender to U.S. forces. In giving himself up, he negotiated the liberation of nearly 100 women and children who were enslaved in the settlements of New Mexico, the largest release of its kind.

Delgadito went on to sign the Treaty of 1868 with the United States, which secured the return of the Diné and the sovereignty of their government. On top of all that, he ran a clandestine counterfeiting operation while imprisoned at Bosque Redondo, duplicating thousands of military ration tickets at a time of mass starvation. He was a remarkable man who saved many lives.

EW: Let's talk about the enslavement of the Navajo people. How did this come to be and what policies of the United States government led to this horrific outcome?

MF: The practice of taking captives originated in warfare. Sometimes captives would be exchanged in prisoner swaps, sometimes they would be kept as slaves. This went on as far back as anyone remembers, and the practice was not limited to the colonial powers. It was the colonizers, however, who turned slavery into an industry, starting with Spain and continuing under Mexican and American rule.

Instead of captives being a byproduct of raids, captives became the whole point of raids. Settlers formed slaving parties and set out for Navajo country, returning with women and children to be sold as household servants. Slavery was never legal in New Mexico Territory, but it was accepted at every level of society. Captives were bought and sold on an almost daily basis. This continued under American rule, reaching its peak in the 1860s.

You asked about U.S policy—there really wasn't any, at least at the national level. All the focus at that time was on slavery in the South, an issue that was already tearing the country apart. Federal officials needed the support of settlers in New Mexico, so they turned a blind eye toward the enslavement of Indigenous people there. In fact, they treated the Navajo as the aggressor, warning them to leave the settlers alone. A handful of Americans working in Navajo country, like Henry Dodge and John Greiner, tried to sound the alarm. They warned Washington that there could be no peace so long as Diné children were being abducted and sold into slavery. But Washington did not listen.

EW: Much of what occurred in your book took place during and shortly after the Civil War. What difference did contemporary Americans see between enslaving African Americans versus Indigenous peoples?

MF: That depends on the individual. Opinions diverged even within the Union Army. At one extreme stood Kit Carson, who personally held three Native youths in servitude. Six months after President Lincoln signed the Emancipation Proclamation, Carson was still paying his mercenaries with captured women and children. He argued that one of the "benefits" of slavery was it would speed the destruction of the Dinés' collective identity.

On the other hand, we have Sam Tappan, the commander of Fort Garland. He condemned that sort of hypocrisy, going so far as to formally accuse a U.S. Indian agent of complicity in the slave trade. Tappan had fought with Carson against the Confederates; Carson even presented Tappan with an engraved saber to commemorate the Union victory at Glorieta Pass. Yet when it came to Indigenous slavery, they couldn't have been farther apart.

Carson's defenders usually fall back on the "presentism" argument, accusing his critics of unfairly judging him by modern standards. But that doesn't really hold up, because Sam Tappan was just as appalled by Indigenous slavery in 1863 as we are today.

EW: Why is this history not remembered by many outside of the Navajo Nation today?

MF: Because it hasn't been taught outside the Navajo Nation. That's a shame, because as tragic as it is, it's also a story of strength and resilience. We have transcripts of hearings and meetings at Bosque Redondo, and they show how the Diné stood up for themselves. They refused to kowtow to the soldiers, even after years of internment. And no matter how bad things got, they always looked out for each other. If everyone were so attentive to the needs of the young, the sick, and the old, I think the world would be a better place.

EW: How is the story of "Old Pounder" and the Navajo slave trade remembered today by the Navajo people?

MF: After Bosque Redondo, Delgadito returned to his forge, leaving governance to Barboncito, Manuelito, and others. I think that's why he's remembered more for silversmithing than for what he did during the Long Walk. Or maybe that's just human nature, to remember the beautiful, and forget the awful. Most Navajo families have Long Walk stories of their own. There was no shortage of heroes in those days. I hope the book draws more attention to what Delgadito achieved, and all the lives he saved. I'm friends with two of his descendants, and they are rightly proud of him.

As for the slave trade, I think it's not just a matter of remembering, but reckoning, and that's an ongoing process for us all. Long buried stories are finally emerging. Folks who grew up calling themselves Hispano are learning they had Indigenous great-great-grandmothers. In southern Colorado, Fort Garland Museum and Cultural Center has been hosting community workshops to help people grapple with these revelations. In Santa Fe, a new research center just opened called Native Bound Unbound, which is creating a digital archive of the Indigenous enslaved, name by name. Hidden histories are being recovered. It's exciting and humbling to think how much more there is to learn.

EW: Did the United States Government ever acknowledge wrongdoing in this tragedy?

MF: Yes. In 1868, the U.S. did something unprecedented—it agreed to give the Navajo back their land. Some of it, at least. The Civil War Gen. William Sherman, hardly considered a soft touch, was personally moved by the plight of the Navajo. During treaty negotiations, Sherman told Barboncito, "All people love the country where they were born and raised. We want to do what is right." Military officers today study what went wrong, to better understand how biases doomed the Army's entrance into Navajo country. In the book I quote an Army historian, Lt. Col. Patrick Naughton, comparing the complexity of the operating environment back then to modern theaters such as Iraq and Afghanistan. So, these are important lessons.

EW: What challenges did you face in your research for *The Counterfeiters of Bosque Redondo*?

MF: Trust was a big one. To tell this story, I needed the help of Diné oral historians. Many are suspicious of non-Native writers, and who can blame them, given all the past distortions. Overcoming that reticence took time. Another challenge was brevity since my publisher set a limit of 40,000 words. That's not a ton of space, and I had a lot of ground to cover. The funny thing is, I ended up grateful for the word-count cap. It kept the story from sprawling out in too many directions. I went over the limit, but not by much, considering the book encompasses three empires, two wars, and the birth of an art form.

Acknowledgements

My gratitude must first go to everyone who agreed over the past several years to be interviewed for *The Tombstone Epitaph* or the Wild West History Association *Journal*. Many of these historians did so graciously when I failed at time management and needed to rush them through the process. Without them none of this would have been possible. I must also thank Mark Boardman of *The Tombstone Epitaph* and Roy Young, retired editor of the Wild West History Association *Journal* who not only eagerly agreed to allow these interviews to be published, but initially saw the value in them when they first saw print. Both are fine men who have helped to guide me into being a better historian and, I hope, someone who can fill their shoes one day. Nods must also be given to the many publicity managers at the various university presses for helping me to make contact with some of these historians. I dare not name them all here for fear of leaving someone out, but Katie Baker at the University of Oklahoma Press, Sarah Dozier at the South Dakota Historical Society Press, Mary Reynolds at the University of Arizona Press, Rosemary Sekora at the University of Nebraska Press, and Bess Whitby at the University of North Texas Press have been invaluable partners in helping to promote the history of the West.

Others include Stuart Rosebrook of *True West* magazine, Melinda Tuey of *The Tombstone Epitaph*, Tonya Barnes of the Greene County Public Library in Paragould, Arkansas, Steven Danver of *Journal of the West*, Robert Clark of the Oregon-California Trails Association *Journal* and my friends and colleagues in the field; many of whom are featured in this book. The last words go to my beloved wife, Laura, and our children Lexie and Jensen. With love, always…

About the Author

Erik J. Wright is the assistant editor of *The Tombstone Epitaph* and a contributing editor for *True West* Magazine. He has written several books on Western history as well as the history of Paragould, Arkansas. His other work has appeared widely in: *Journal of the West*, *True West* magazine, *Wild West* magazine, *The Tombstone Epitaph*, the Wild West History Association *Journal*, the Oregon-California Trails Association *Journal*, *The Bounty* magazine, and others.

He is the winner of the 2016 Wild West History Association prize for Best Feature Article in a Western History Magazine, 12 Arkansas Press Association Awards, and was the 2021 recipient of the Lola M. Homsher Research Grant presented by the Wyoming State Historical Society.

Wright is an active member of the Wild West History Association, the English Westerners' Society, the Pitcairn and Norfolk Islands Society, Wyoming State Historical Society, and the Oregon-California Trails Association.

He lives in northeast Arkansas with his wife and two children.

www.erikwrighthistorian.com

Made in the USA
Columbia, SC
23 December 2023